The Soul *of* Apologetics

The Soul *of* Apologetics

A Spiritual Companion *for* Defenders *of the* Faith

© 2025 Catholic Answers

All rights reserved. Except for quotations, no part of this book may be reproduced or transmitted in any form or by any means, electronic or mechanical, including photocopying, recording, uploading to the internet, or by any information storage and retrieval system without written permission from the publisher.

Unless otherwise noted, Scripture texts in this work are taken from the *New American Bible, revised edition* © 2010, 1991, 1986, 1970 Confraternity of Christian Doctrine, Washington, D.C. and are used by permission of the copyright owner. All Rights Reserved. No part of the New American Bible may be reproduced in any form without permission in writing from the copyright owner.

Published by Catholic Answers, Inc.
2020 Gillespie Way
El Cajon, California 92020
1-888-291-8000 orders
619-387-0042 fax
catholic.com

Printed in the United States of America

Interior design by Maria L.T. Bowman
Cover design by eBookLaunch.com

978-1-68357-368-5
978-1-68357-369-2 Kindle
978-1-68357-370-8 ePub

✠ Direct, O Lord, all our actions
   by your holy inspirations,
     and carry them on by your gracious assistance.
     So that every prayer and work of ours
     may begin always with you,
     and by you be happily ended.

Contents

Introduction A Religion of the Heart ix

1 God's Existence and Nature 1

2 God's Good Creation 41

3 God Comes to His People. 91

4 Christ's Body, the Church 143

Conclusion The Soul of Apologetics 195

Works Cited in this Book 205

Prayer Index 209

INTRODUCTION

A Religion of the Heart

Christian apologetics arose during a time of persecution in the 200s . . . and not much has changed between then and the 2000s.

What Rome started then, the secular culture continues now, but often in even more vile and vicious ways. Whereas a person living in the second century was utterly convinced that something numinous governed the universe and that truth was both discoverable and demanding, modern man mocks both of those realities: *if* there is a god, he must be a moral monster for allowing so much suffering in the world, and *if* there is truth, it's a purely personal preference or just part of a power grab by those with an agenda.

The early Church battled heresies that were trying to lay false claim to the privilege of being called Catholic. Today, Catholics are under continual barrage from Christian and quasi-Christian sects that want them to exchange their received apostolic faith for the novelties of the Reformation and its offspring.

And where the first generations of Christian leaders had to struggle to rise above pagan immorality and live according to the new way of Christ, today we must resist a new paganism—while dealing with the scandals of corrupted leaders, half-hearted disciples, and bad theology that hinder our efforts to spread the gospel.

Today, as then, we who wish to defend and spread the Faith must proceed with love and patience, as we instruct the ignorant, repel the attacks of Catholicism's detractors, and give a compelling witness of Christian joy to the modern world's apathetic masses.

All this requires more than the right arguments, prooftexts, and citations. It requires *grace*. It requires an integration of our mind and spirit, each suffused with charity. To be a light in the darkness of the world, today as in every age, we must root apologetics and evangelization deeply in prayer. Our reading and study and practice are the mind of apologetics. Our interior disposition is its *soul*.

Cultivating this disposition begins, of course, with liturgical prayer and the efficacious sacraments. It includes family and personal prayer, reflection and mediation on the mysteries, the pursuit of private devotions, and every other salutary Christian spiritual practice. This book in your hands falls in this category but is a specialized kind of tool, ordered to the mental and spiritual fortifications we need to be effective witnesses to and defenders of the Faith.

Those fortifications are of three kinds. First, there is the consideration of perhaps-familiar apologetics data and arguments, but with special attention to their spiritual, salvific meaning. Secondly, there is reflection on the apologist's duty not just to the truth but to other souls; that is, on apologetics as a work of charity. Finally, there is the effort to grow within our hearts the apostolic virtues without which no apologist or evangelist can be successful. Love, patience, zeal, magnanimity,

The Twin Pillars of Love and Truth

humility—these are indispensable but hardly natural, and they require ardent training to achieve and maintain.

Many of us know that famous passage in St. Peter's first epistle where he exhorts us always to "prepared to make a defense to anyone who calls you to account for the hope that is in you" (1 Pet. 3:15). Fewer, perhaps, know the words that follow: "yet do it with gentleness and reverence." This verse is the biblical charter for all would-be apologists!

The lesser-known preceding verse, though, shows that the first pope understood that the gentle, reverent work of apologetics out in the world begins with our inner life. To those who find themselves in a culture that requires a defense against doubters and persecutors (that is us!) he says, "In your hearts reverence Christ as Lord." And so, he builds the *duty of explaining our reasons* upon our *striving for sanctity*.

Apologetics, then, is built upon the two pillars of love and truth, rooted in reverence for the Lord. For holiness without truth is empty piety or emotion-soothing; truth without holiness is only worldly one-upmanship, the need to feel superior by winning an argument. (St. Thomas called this the sin of *contention*.) If we set out to defend and explain the Faith but separate love from truth, we will fail. This book is meant to foster success in your apologetics efforts, then, not by teaching you fresh new arguments but by helping you to ground all those efforts in prayer and reflection.

THE SIGN OF THE CROSS

✠ In the name of the Father, and of the Son, and of the Holy Spirit. Amen.

How This Book Works

This prayer book is divided into four main sections. The first looks at the existence and nature of God. The second explores the gift of creation and the glory of the human person. Then we treat the coming of Jesus and the Holy Spirit. And finally, we arrive at Christ's Church. Each section will begin with a fitting prayer and then the purpose of such an apologetic.

Christ and the faith he gave us are the only perfect target for the longing of the human heart. Christianity is not just one creed among many; it is exactly what *every person* ever was created to desire and pursue. It is the *universal* (in Greek, "catholic") and timeless way of life because only love can satisfy what we have been created for.

Recognizing Christianity as the religion of the heart, we can note in our four sections four guiding themes essential for today's apologetics.

First, *every human person wants to love and to be loved*. Love alone can produce the joy that transcends the inevitable hurdles of life. Love is God's very nature, and as we reflect on love and what love has revealed, we learn not only that God exists but that he is a Trinity. In our first section we will prayerfully examine the more traditional proofs for God's existence as well as some insights into the Christian view of God as the Creator and Sustainer of all that is.

A second theme begins with the question, *"What does such love do?"* Here we shall draw from the traditional twofold answer given by philosophers and theologians over the centuries: (1) love works to secure the good of the other and (2) love longs to be in the beloved's presence. This second section will therefore examine the way love has created us in a world of gifts. The benevolence we see in God's providence is the first characteristic of charity; so we shall take up themes of God's creation of the human person and his endowing us with so many unique and unmatchable gifts.

The third section looks at the next characteristic of love—what it means to *desire to be in the presence of one's beloved*. Love not only wants to give and receive gifts; it longs to share its very self. Every lover knows this: an unavoidable mark of love is *union*. Because love longs to draw near to the beloved, we shall use section three to focus on the ultimate gift of God's sending his only begotten Son and, in turn, his sending us his Holy Spirit.

Fourthly, *communion is marked by joy*. An other-centered life shared with generosity produces conviviality. That is why our final section will treat the nature of Christ's Church, along with the sacraments and the saints who receive them. In this context we shall also look at what it means to serve the holy ones of God in works of mercy. And then, since all lovers hope for a future together in which their love defeats all things, we shall conclude by examining the four last things: the Catholic understanding of death, judgment, hell, and heaven.

Christ tells us that he is not just a way but *the* way (John 14:6). Christianity is not a tru-ism but *the* truth. Christ is not just someone alive like us; he is *the* life who makes all men and women truly live. As you read this book, ask Christ to guide you on his way and fill you with his life. Ask him to send his Holy Spirit to lead you through these pages as a kind of retreat. Bring before the Lord your past experiences—successes and failures—in defending and explaining the Faith, and offer to him all the future opportunities he will give you.

THE *GLORY BE*

✠ Glory be to the Father, and to the Son, and
to the Holy Spirit.

As it was in the beginning, is now, and ever shall
be, world without end.

The elements in this book include various prayers suited to the apologetic theme that are meant to orient both your mind and heart to what God hopes to deepen within you. You will also discover prayerful selections from the liturgy, edifying passages from many Church Fathers and Doctors, and insights from saintly Christian writers over the centuries. While reading, as you feel so moved, dwell on those prayers and wise reflections, lifting your soul to God and asking him to bring spiritual fruit from them.

Jesus' disciples knew that prayer could be taught and that the Master himself was the one to show them the best way to pray: "He was praying in a certain place, and when he had finished, one of his disciples said to him, '*Lord, teach us to pray* just as John taught his disciples'" (Luke 11:1). It's true that prayer can be very simple and brief, at times nothing more than small gestures of praise or trust or docility. But prayer is also a discipline, a practice that can be taught, learned, and improved with diligent attention.

> Prayer is the raising of one's mind and heart to
> God or the requesting of good things from God.
>
> — ST. JOHN DAMASCENE

Parts of This Book

> For me, prayer is a surge of the heart; it is a simple look turned toward heaven, it is a cry of recognition and of love, embracing both trial and joy.
>
> — ST. THÉRÈSE OF LISIEUX

> If you are not successful in prayer, you will not be successful in anything, for prayer is the foundation of everything.
>
> — ST. THEOPHAN THE RECLUSE

We don't have to build this foundation of prayer ourselves! In fact, by ourselves we are too weak to do it. But the Holy Spirit is not. So, ask him now to aid you, as St. Paul assures us:

> In the same way, the Spirit too comes to the aid of our weakness; for we do not know how to pray as we ought, but the Spirit himself intercedes with inexpressible groanings. And the one who searches hearts knows what is the intention of the Spirit, because he intercedes for the holy ones according to God's will.
>
> — ROMANS 8:26–27

You might consider sitting with these pages prayerfully before the Blessed Sacrament or immediately following the celebration of Mass when the graces of Holy Communion are most immediate; or at least as part of some regular routine each morning, afternoon, or evening. In any case, try to use this book in a contemplative place where you can stop, be still, and ponder what the Spirit of God desires to say to you. You might also wish to keep a small journal by your side to write down any thoughts, resolutions, or reminders as your prayer period unfolds.

> I want a laity, not arrogant, not rash in speech, not disputatious, but men who know their religion, who enter into it, who know just where they stand, who know what they hold, and what they do not, who know their creed so well, that they can give an account of it, who know so much of history that they can defend it.
>
> I want an intelligent, well-instructed laity . . . I wish you to enlarge your knowledge, to cultivate your reason, to get an insight into the relation of truth to truth, to learn to view things as they are, to understand how faith and reason stand to each other, what are the bases and principles of Catholicism, and where lie the main inconsistencies and absurdities of the Protestant theory.
>
> — ST. JOHN HENRY NEWMAN

1

God's Existence and Nature

> For what can be known about God is evident to them, because God made it evident to them. Ever since the creation of the world, his invisible attributes of eternal power and divinity have been able to be understood and perceived in what he has made. As a result, they have no excuse.
>
> — ROMANS 1:19–20

God has no beginning, but we do—and with him we should always begin (and end . . . and be ever sustained by!). This is why our first section aims to achieve two objectives: first, to review the classic proofs for God's existence in a prayerful way, and second, to see why God-as-love is the fundamental truth upon which all other truths depend. In this way we shall move from *what* God is to *who* he is as Father, Son, and Holy Spirit.

Have you always just taken God's existence for granted? Many others do not. Some struggle with the problem of evil—how a seemingly good God could overlook the cruelties obvious in every news report around the globe. Some have had "God" used as a justification for the coldness or even the viciousness poured out upon them. Let us be careful not to judge doubters and risk losing the opportunity to lay out for them that God does in fact exist.

Catholics begin worship by admitting our sinfulness and need for grace. To begin this spiritual study, we might similarly reflect on the obstacles that keep us from effectively defending the Faith. Some struggle with pride. Others lack confidence in their knowledge or skills and faith in God's ability to work through them. What are three biases or bad habits that stand in *your* way?

PRAYER OF THOMAS À KEMPIS

✠ Grant me, O Lord, to know what I ought to know, to love what I ought to love, to praise what delights thee most, to value what is precious in thy sight, to hate what is offensive to thee. Do not suffer me to judge according to the sight of my eyes, nor to pass sentence according to the hearing of the ears of ignorant men; but to discern with a true judgment between things visible and spiritual, and above all, always to inquire what is the good pleasure of thy will.

God Reveals Himself Through Head and Heart

Divine revelation tells us that God is both the essence of all that is real *and* a community of charity—one divine nature in three divine Persons. The first part can be confirmed through the use of human reason (*that* God is), whereas we only know the latter because God chose to reveal it to us (*who* God is). The first is to affirm, through intelligence and experience, that there must exist a Being who is uncaused and wholly and fully real; the second is to receive, as a gift, a supra-rational insight about the nature of love as it is perfectly realized in that Being.

To know God in such a manner—both Love and Lover—combines the heart of Jewish theology with the mind of Greek philosophy. For God's first chosen people, Yahweh was a God who entered into covenants, who proved faithful even when his people rejected him. God was someone with whom you could have a personal connection built on fidelity and intimacy. For the Greeks, on the other hand, the divine was not someone with whom you could have an "I-you" relationship but was instead the ultimate concentration or essence of the good, the true, and the beautiful.

How do we prepare to share this full truth of our heart-and-mind God? Well, for us humans the existence of *anything* is verifiable in one of only two ways: either we have *immediate sense experience* of it, or we *infer its existence* through its direct effects.

For example, we can know that our next-door neighbor has a dog by seeing the new pup or hearing its bark all night. But we can also know by taking note of the new doghouse in the neighbor's yard, or by the holes it dug to bury bones. Both ways tell us of the dog's existence—the first immediately and directly, the second from the effects of a dog's presence.

In this life, no human experiences direct sense experience of God. Our proofs for God's existence, then, must follow the second way of knowing. We work with what we *can* know directly, and then follow it back to its cause.

TO KNOW AND LOVE GOD

✠ God, it may be true that I do not know you
as well as I could.
It is true that I do not love you
as much as you deserve.

I grant you permission to remove the
blindness from my eyes,
and to remove the apathy from my heart,
that I may know you as you are known
and to love you as you are loved.

Arguing for and witnessing to God's existence through truths attainable by rational demonstration comes in especially handy when dialoging with the kind of avowed atheists who dismiss religious belief as nothing but feelings and emotion. We must remember, though, that any proof for God is just the beginning of our walk with him. If we approach God *only* through logical propositions and syllogisms, and end there, we will miss his love and mercy.

Accordingly, for the greatest of Catholic minds, St. Thomas Aquinas, the proofs and other introductory truths of the Faith were merely meant to clear away obstacles to make room for the fuller, saving articles of our faith.

God Reveals Himself Through Head and Heart

> The existence of God and other like truths about God, which can be known by natural reason, are not articles of faith, but are preambles to the articles (praeambula fidei); for faith presupposes natural knowledge, even as grace presupposes nature, and perfection supposes something that can be perfected.
>
> — ST. THOMAS AQUINAS

Let us then approach the existence of God with what can be known "by natural reason," keeping in mind that the truth of God is much more—founded upon but transcending anything our senses or logic tell us.

SURRENDER TO GOD

✠ Loving God, although I cannot yet see you as you are,
I am surrounded by all the effects of
your love and power.
I surrender my eyes to you so I may see you in and
through all that is.
I surrender my mind to you that I may be aware of
you in and through all that is.
I surrender my heart to you that I may
swell with gratitude
by understanding you and your ways more thankfully.

Almighty God, my eternal Father, from this fullness,
I ask that you grant me the grace to live
this life ever more awake to you and all your
laborings on my behalf.

Direct my entire self, that it may be attuned to you in
body, mind, and soul,
sensing you in all that is, understanding you
through all you have done,
and loving you for all that you are.

Saint Thomas Aquinas's Five Ways

Each of Aquinas's five famous proofs for God's existence depends on the indisputable metaphysical fact that a chain of caused (or "contingent") beings *cannot go on forever*. Such an "infinite regress" of caused causes or designed creatures is simply logically impossible. And since we live in a world of wonderful and elaborately designed beings which clearly come in and out of existence, therefore there *must* exist a causer and designer whose existence does not change or depend on anything else in order to exist.

PRAYER FOR STUDENTS

St. Thomas Aquinas

✠ Creator of all things, true source of light and wisdom, origin of all being,

graciously let a ray of your light penetrate the
darkness of my understanding.
Take from me the double darkness in
which I have been born,
an obscurity of sin and ignorance.

Give me a keen understanding, a retentive memory,
and the ability to grasp things
correctly and fundamentally.
Grant me the talent of being
exact in my explanations
and the ability to express myself with
thoroughness and charm.

Point out the beginning, direct the progress, and
help in the completion.
I ask this through Christ our Lord.

Motion

The *first way* St. Thomas shows how this must be is to focus our attention on the fact that things that change or move from one state to another cannot change themselves. Tinder catches fire only through the application of heat or a spark; the water in a lake will only rise or fall depending on the rain or sunshine it encounters. The word *motion* to describe this way does not mean "locomotion," then, but an ability to proceed from one state into another; and clearly, *everything* in our world is in this kind of constant motion.

If all things we experience are in this caused motion, and the causes can't regress infinitely, what was the *first* thing to "move" something else? Whatever it is, it cannot itself have been moved by something else. We have just inferred the existence of the Unmoved Mover.

Cause

St. Thomas's second proof is much like the first, but it instead highlights the fact that nothing can *cause* itself to exist. Everything we can observe was made to be by some external agent. Our parents brought us into being, and the same could be said about every animal, plant, and every artifact that could not cause itself to be.

And since those causes can't logically go back in an infinite chain, we can reach the conclusion that there must be a first cause that is not caused by anything else. There must be one being whose essence it is to exist. There cannot be a Big Bang without a "Big Banger"!

This proof invokes what is called the *efficient* cause, one of four kinds of cause identified by Aristotle:

- Material Cause: that *out of which* something comes
- Formal Cause: that *which* something is
- Efficient Cause: that *by which* something comes
- Final Cause: that *for which* something is

Here we can pause and reflect on our own four causes:

Material: Let us be grateful for the man and woman who helped bring us into existence, and remember that our body has been consecrated into a spiritual temple (1 Cor. 6:19–20). *Do we truly see how we treat our body as part of our Christian discipleship?*

Formal: Our souls are unending, given to us by the Eternal One himself. *What do we put into this soul through our senses? Do we think about what is above (Col. 3:2) or do we bombard our souls with images, pleasures, stresses, and anxieties of this fallen world?*

Efficient: In the act of procreation, our fathers and mothers cooperated with God to make us who we uniquely are—an irreplaceable and immortal human person with a body and soul. *Do we struggle to live an integrated life of body and soul, heaven and earth?*

Final: Like everything else, we have an ultimate purpose! We are not random appendages on the universe. *Are we able to discern wisely how to order our intermediate ends (career, daily duties, etc.) with our ultimate end? How can we make choices that align better with the purpose for which God created us?*

For in him we live and move and have our being.

— ACTS 17:28

Potentiality and Necessity

St. Thomas's third proof draws from another fact of our experience: that no one thing we ever encounter *has* to exist. To put it in philosophical language, we have never met anyone or interacted with anything whose essence (*what* a thing is) includes its existence (*that* a thing is). The most obvious and universal sorrow in this world is the reality that everything eventually fades and goes away—loved ones leave, flowers and pets and parents die; and all things teeter on the edge of potentiality.

Yet if absolutely *everything* were potential, nothing at all would exist. Since we know that things exist, we can infer the existence of one ultimate being who is not potential but is unbounded Necessity. God told Moses as much when he revealed himself as "I am who am" (Exod. 3:14). To put the exchange another way: Moses asked God, "What is your essence?" and God said, "My essence is existence."

GOD'S GRANDEUR

The world is charged with the grandeur of God.
  It will flame out, like shining from shook foil;
  It gathers to a greatness, like the ooze of oil
Crushed. Why do men then now not reck his rod?
Generations have trod, have trod, have trod;
  And all is seared with trade;
bleared, smeared with toil;
  And wears man's smudge and shares
man's smell: the soil
Is bare now, nor can foot feel, being shod.

The Five Ways

And for all this, nature is never spent;
There lives the dearest freshness deep down things;
And though the last lights off the black West went
Oh, morning, at the brown
brink eastward, springs —
Because the Holy Ghost over the bent
World broods with warm breast
and with ah! bright wings.

— GERARD MANLEY HOPKINS

Gradation

The fourth way recognizes how we all naturally judge things against each other: we perceive that some things are better or shinier or hotter or heavier than others. We do this even without always realizing or applying an objective standard. Do we all not have an implicit "scale" in our minds that weighs things—a song, a sunset, a burrito—against others that our senses experience?

This being the case, Aquinas argues that there can't be such grades of goodness or perfection unless there existed some (however undefined or imaginable) "best" or pre-eminent being in mind. Without an ultimate Best to calibrate the cosmic scale, there could be no real gradations. Since we perceive that there are, the ultimate Best must exist and we call him God.

Design

Aquinas's fifth and final way is based on our perception that things around us act for an intelligible end. We speak of the "laws of nature" by which the sensible universe behaves in an ordered and predictable way—the very basis of all our human science and technology. If we perceive laws, St. Thomas says, it is rational to conclude that there is a law-maker. Where there is design, there is a designer. Who or what is the Inventor, Initiator, or Grand Schemer behind the intricate universe that presents itself to our reason? St. Thomas argues that it must be a designer whose designs depend on nothing other than his own nature; an intelligence not needing anything else for its order but on which all the universe's order rests.

TO DO GOD'S WILL
Attributed to St. Thomas Aquinas

✠ O Merciful God, grant that I may ever perfectly do
your will in all things.
Let it be my ambition to work only for
your honor and glory.

Let me rejoice in nothing but what leads to you,
nor grieve for anything that leads away from you.

May all passing things be as nothing in my eyes,
and may all that is yours be dear to me,
and you, my God, dear above them all.

Our Longing for Happiness

May all joy be meaningless without you
and may I desire nothing apart from you.
May all labor and toil delight me when it is for you.

Make me, O Lord, obedient without complaint,
poor without regret, patient without murmur,
humble without pretense, joyous without frivolity,
and truthful without disguise.

Give me, O God, an ever-watchful heart
which nothing can ever lure away from you;
a noble heart, which no unworthy affection
can draw downwards to the earth;
an unconquerable heart, which no evil can warp;
an unconquerable heart, which no
tribulation can crush;
a free heart, which no perverted affection
can claim for its own.

Bestow on me, O God, understanding to know you,
diligence to seek you, and wisdom to find you;
a life which may please you, and a hope which may
embrace you at the last.

There is another way of approaching God's existence while relying on the natural lights of human reasoning alone. This *psychological argument* proceeds by noting the "space" in all human experience between where we are and where we know we should be.

It begins by observing how we are surrounded by inanimate and non-rational things that cannot help but do what they do: rocks tumble down a hill, leaves blow in the wind, cats chase mice. To some extent we are no different. We succumb to hunger and thirst, are subject to gravity and time, and so on. But we also live in the world of *moral possibilities*—things that aren't determined, but "ought" to happen in one way or another.

We may be tired, but we still *ought* to fulfill the duties of my state in life. We may be hungry, but we still *ought not* to punch a stranger and take his hamburger. We may find the man or woman across the street attractive, but we ought to be faithful to our spouse and ought not to woo someone else's. These "oughts" are not expected of lower creatures.

This portrait helps to confirm Aquinas's arguments, especially his fifth way. But it also introduces a new component. This world of duty, morality, and ideals forces us to recognize there is a law hovering over me that expects or obliges me to act in a certain way. I am free to dismiss that law and do what I ought not, but that usually comes at my own sad peril.

Where there is such an effect, there must be an equal or higher cause, and we call that cause—that great giver of oughts—"God."

A variation on this psychological approach is to focus not on our natural awareness of moral duty but on our natural desire for *happiness*. It, too, needs a cause.

Our Longing for Happiness

What do you long for? Do you define joy differently from happiness? How so? How do you imagine heaven and what do you think will open those gates for you?

> Creatures are not born with desires unless satisfaction for those desires exists. A baby feels hunger: well, there is such a thing as food. A duckling wants to swim: well, there is such a thing as water. Men feel sexual desire: well, there is such a thing as sex. If I find in myself a desire which no experience in this world can satisfy, the most probable explanation is that I was made for another world . . . .
>
> I must keep alive in myself the desire for my true country, which I shall not find till after death; I must never let it get snowed under or turned aside; I must make it the main object of life to press on to that other country and to help others to do the same.
>
> — C.S. LEWIS

We cannot help but desire happiness—even when, because of our sin-darkened intellects, we mis-identify what will bring it to us. This universal human urge is another effect that demands a cause. If we find ourselves restless and unsatisfied through so much of this life while still yearning for a tranquility without end, from where might that desire for unalloyed happiness come? God is both its giver and fulfillment.

THE SOUL OF APOLOGETICS

To know that God exists in a general and confused way is implanted in us by nature, inasmuch as God is man's beatitude. For man naturally desires happiness, and what is naturally desired by man must be naturally known to him. This, however, is not to know absolutely that God exists; just as to know that someone is approaching is not the same as to know that Peter is approaching, even though it is Peter who is approaching; for many there are who imagine that man's perfect good which is happiness, consists in riches, and others in pleasures, and others in something else.

— ST. THOMAS AQUINAS

Do you remember when you came to realize that God alone could bring you happiness? Where in life were you when you understood how no creature, however beautiful, could fulfill your soul, but that in God you and other creatures could love each other even more? What are the gifts through which he bestows his joy upon you and upon others through you?

REGINA COELI

✠ Queen of Heaven, rejoice, *alleluia*.
   For he, whom you did merit to bear, *alleluia*.
   Has risen as he said, *alleluia*.
   Pray for us to God, *alleluia*.

Than Which Nothing Greater Can Be Conceived

Rejoice and be glad, O Virgin Mary, *alleluia*.
For the Lord is truly risen, *alleluia*.

Let us pray: O God, who gave joy to the world through the resurrection of thy Son, our Lord Jesus Christ, grant we beseech thee, that through the intercession of the Virgin Mary, his mother, we may obtain the joys of everlasting life. Through the same Christ our Lord.

A medieval monk and saint named Anselm of Canterbury offered a different way of arriving at the conclusion that there has to be a God.

First, he said, we can all agree that to exist both in the mind as well as in reality is greater than to exist in the mind alone. Would you not rather have one real dollar than a million mental dollars? So, if we think of God as (in Anselm's words) "a being than which no greater can be conceived"—and he surely must be—then he must exist in reality, because to exist in reality is greater than just to be conceived in our thoughts.

The main objection to this way of thinking was posed by a colleague of Anselm's, who argued that if it is better to exist both in the mind and in reality than in just the mind, must we then not posit the existence of the best of all tropical islands, steins of the best possible beer, the most beautiful of landscapes, and so on? But this is to miss the point, replies Anselm: this "ontological proof," as it came to be called, works only for "the greatest possible being." Only such a being *must* include all perfections.

Anselm's proof, though considered eccentric by some today, has provided grounds for rich reflection for nearly nine centuries.

PRAYER OF ST. ANSELM

✠ Oh my God, teach my heart where and how to seek
you, where and how to find you.
You are my God and you are my all and I
have never seen you.
You have made me and remade me,
You have bestowed on me all the
good things I possess.
Still I do not know you.

I have not yet done that for which I was made.
Teach me to seek you.
I cannot seek you unless you teach me or find you
unless you show yourself to me.
Let me seek you in my desire, let me
desire you in my seeking.
Let me find you by loving you, let me love
you when I find you.

The Wager

We will look at one more proof, but it is more like a bet. Which makes sense, because it comes from the philosopher/mathematician who invented the roulette wheel.

Blaise Pascal's famous "wager" is on whether or not God exists, and he says it makes much more sense to "bet" on God and go through life as if he does.

The logic of the wager is simple. The diehard atheist, who spends his entire life as if there is no God, gains nothing if he's right but *loses everything* if he's wrong. But the person who bets on God, and lives his life accordingly, loses nothing if he's wrong but *gains everything* if he's right.

"I refuse to wager" is not an option, because simply by living and choosing every day, as we all inch toward death and a potential reckoning for our lives, we are all already and inescapably wagering. We *have to* play this game, and the only way to win is by betting there is a God.

When Pascal died on August 18, 1662, he was wearing a coat with a prayer sewn into its lining—a prayer and a transformative memory he recalled often and prayed constantly throughout the day.

> Monday, 23 November, feast of St. Clement, pope
> and martyr, and others in the martyrology.
> Vigil of St. Chrysogonus, martyr,
> and others. From about half past ten at night
> until about half past midnight,
>
> FIRE.
>
> God of Abraham, God of Isaac, God of Jacob,
> not of the philosophers and of the learned.
> Certitude. Certitude. Feeling. Joy. Peace.

THE SOUL OF APOLOGETICS

God of Jesus Christ.
My God and your God.
your God will be my God.
Forgetfulness of the world and of
everything, except God.
He is only found by the ways taught in the gospel.
Grandeur of the human soul.
Righteous Father, the world has not known you,
but I have known you.
Joy, joy, joy, tears of joy.
I have departed from him:
They have forsaken me, the fount of living water.
My God, will you leave me?
Let me not be separated from him forever.
This is eternal life, that they know you, the one true
God, and the one that you sent, Jesus Christ.
Jesus Christ.
Jesus Christ.
I left him; I fled him, renounced, crucified.
Let me never be separated from him.
He is only kept securely by the ways
taught in the gospel:
Renunciation, total and sweet.
Complete submission to Jesus
Christ and to my director.
Eternally in joy for a day's exercise on the earth.
Not to forget your words.

— BLAISE PASCAL

Conscience and the Commandments

As compelling and useful such proofs for God's existence might be, we need to remember: we don't pray to an Uncaused Cause or lay down our life for the sake of an Unmoved Mover. And "wagering" belief on a deity just because the odds favor it doesn't make saints. Our love of God must go deeper than the logic of proofs. God wants those whose minds yield to the rigor of his truth *and* whose hearts melt before the gentleness of his love. The central image of Christianity is not an equation but a broken, crucified man.

As we approach the one true God, we must begin to notice how we, at some level of our psyches, do not really want to be *too* near. The Old Testament saints were quite adamant that only the pure can come into contact with the Lord's awful majesty. All that is unclean and evil must be purged from his midst (Deut. 13:5–6).

To approach the living God means that we must be open to being made as godlike as possible; for us fallen creatures, that is to admit our need to be purged of our sins. Perhaps, in our modern therapeutic culture, we have lost sight of our unworthiness to approach God. At every Holy Communion, however, Catholics are prompted to remind themselves as the Roman soldier did: "Lord, I am not worthy that you should enter under my roof."

Examination of Conscience to Prepare for the Presence of the Lord

I am the Lord your God: you shall not have strange gods before me: Who, really, is the G/god in my life? Do I give more time to my finances, my social life, my enjoyment of good things than I do to God and the things of God, such as prayer, study, and the almsdeeds?

You shall not take the name of the Lord your God in vain: Do I use the Lord's name in times of anger or frustration? Do I give scandal to others with the way I speak of God and his Church?

Remember to keep holy the Lord's day: How is the Sabbath at all different than the other days of my week? Do I faithfully and prayerfully attend Mass on Sundays as well as holy days of obligation? Do I strive alter my work schedule or leisure plans to keep the Mass precept?

Honor your father and your mother: Have I shown my parents the proper respect due to them? If they are deceased, do I pray for them and continue even now to thank them for the gift of life and so many other blessings bestowed on me through their care? Am I able to forgive them for any mistakes, myself now knowing parents do the best they can?

You shall not kill: Have I ever harmed another or been complicit in the taking of human life? Do I "kill" through verbal or emotional abuse, through the sins of calumny or detraction, enjoying salacious gossip more than the truth of things?

You shall not commit adultery: If I am married, am I faithful to my spouse in thought, word, and deed? Do I live out my sexuality in accord with Christ's teachings no matter my state in life? Do I engage on sexual sins online? Do I find myself leering at others as sexually exploitative objects and not as beautiful sons and daughters of our Father?

You shall not steal: Have I ever taken anything that I know I should have paid for but did not? Do I "steal" time from my family or employer by wasting it through useless habits or personal distance, whether professionally or emotionally?

You shall not bear false witness against your neighbor: Do I find myself telling lies or telling stories about others in order to make myself look "in the know"? Do I ever fail to tell the truth in order to keep others from knowing what I am up to, where I might be going, or what is truly on my mind?

You shall not covet your neighbor's spouse: Do I lust after others I see, failing to practice custody of the eyes? Do I honor my own husband or wife, pouring myself out for that person with full affection and Christ's own love? Do I ever find myself thinking that other people enjoy better relationships than I do?

You shall not covet your neighbor's goods: Do I find myself constantly stressed about my material situation and therefore envious with what others have? Do I find myself constantly comparing my state in life with those around me?

DELIVERANCE FROM EVIL

✠ Deliver us, we beseech Thee, O Lord, from all evils past, present, and to come: and by the intercession of blessed Mary, ever virgin, and of all the saints, mercifully grant peace in our days, that by the assistance of thy holy grace we may be always free from sin and secure from all disturbance.

When God gives us a command, he is sharing the desires of his heart with us. That is how love works: when your beloved asks a particular something from you, his or her love does not depend on your fulfilling that request. True love is truly unconditional. Yet, how selfishly petty you would be if you were to disregard such a wish. It is that way with God as well: his espoused love does not depend on our fulfilling these commands, but in our fulfilling them we can love God all the more and in the way he has asked. These commands are for *our* flourishing, not his.

In our day and age, too many wrongly believe that law and love are opposed; that "love is love" and that means anything we call "love" is beyond moral judgment. The God of truth, however, does not distinguish between commandment and charity. For acting and thinking in a virtuous manner, as he has commanded, is the sign and seal of love.

Our God commands but he never demands. Instead, he *invites* us to choose the fullness of life, first by putting away all that harms us and then by freely choosing—with the help of this grace—what fulfils and perfects us.

Perfection Personified

> See, I have today set before you life and good, death and evil. If you obey the commandments of the Lord, your God, which I am giving you today, loving the Lord, your God, and walking in his ways, and keeping his commandments, statutes and ordinances, you will live and grow numerous, and the Lord, your God, will bless you in the land you are entering to possess.
>
> — DEUTERONOMY 30:15–16

The self-revelation of a God who would interact in this way began with his first chosen ones. From the brilliance of the Jewish people, and the covenants they made with their one true God, came proof that Yahweh was one with whom you could enter into a relationship—a personal pact—as you would with a parent or friend. In Judaism, the world is introduced to a God who is responsive and caring, selective in his love and providence. This God insisted that he is one and transcendent, yet he offered his people a tender I-thou relationship with him. This is a God unrivaled yet available, universal yet personal.

Christianity inherited not only this understanding of a personal God but received also from Greek philosophy that this same God is the Immutable, the Good, the True, the Beautiful, the essence of all that is real. At the same time able and eager to be personally involved in the lives of his people, this same God was at the same time wholly beyond them and unable to be restrained by anything else. Herein lies the brilliance of Christianity, in our inheritance of both the Jewish God who is a tremendous lover and the Greek philosophical God who is the essence of love.

Later medieval language would say that God is at once both *esse*—existence itself—and *ens*—one who personally exists. Let us now therefore move our attention from God as *esse* to God as *ens*: to his being a Trinity of love and the perfect community of self-gift.

THAT ALL MAY KNOW GOD IN TRUTH
St. Irenaeus

✠ I appeal to you, Lord, God of Abraham, God of Isaac, God of Jacob and Israel,
you the Father of our Lord Jesus Christ.
Infinitely merciful as you are, it is your will that we should learn to know you.
You made heaven and earth; you rule supreme over all that is.
You are the true, the only God; there is no other god above you.

Through our Lord Jesus Christ . . . and the gifts of the Holy Spirit,
grant that all who read what I have written here may know you, because you alone are God;
let them draw strength from you; keep them from all teaching that is heretical, irreligious, or godless.

Perfection Personified

Our reflections so far provide invaluable information about God and his *aseity* (a fancy Latin term denoting total self-sufficiency). Yet no Christian can limit his understanding of God just to the fullness of being, as awesome as that might be. God is not just power; he is also Person; not just existence but One who Exists; not just love but a Lover.

TO BE CONFORMED TO THE HOLY SPIRIT

✠ Omnipotent Father,
 help my frailty
 and rescue me from the depths of ignorance.

Only Wise Son,
 direct all my thoughts, words, and deeds
 to your Sacred Heart.

O Love who is the Holy Spirit,
 be the font and origin of all my mind's
 thoughts and desires,
 that all I think and do may be conformed
 to God's saving pleasure.

To pray this way proves we are no longer natural but supernatural creatures; for in knowing God as three divine Persons in one divine nature we realize we have received his gift of revelation. The unbroken Catholic tradition has always argued that by the use of natural human reason, through philosophy, we can (and should) know *that* God exists. But to know *who* God ultimately *is*, he must choose to tell us.

God reveals his trinitarian life to those adopted children whom he is forming into saints. As a medieval adage puts it, "Only like knows like." Only one who strives for the good can know what goodness is; only the just can understand the real meaning of justice, and so on. St. Basil of Caesarea (330–79), who led the Church's insistence that the Holy Spirit is fully and consubstantially God (at the First Council of Constantinople in 381), co-equal to the Father and the Son, held accordingly that only those who are humble enough to surrender to the self-gift which is the Trinity can understand how the Father and the Son and the Holy Spirit can all be one.

> If we are illumined by divine power, and fix our eyes on the beauty of the image of the invisible God, and through the image are led up to the indescribable beauty of its source, it is because we have been inseparably joined to the spirit of knowledge. He gives those who love the vision of truth the power which enables them to see the image, and this power is himself. He does not reveal it to them from outside sources, but leads them to knowledge personally, "No one knows the Father except the Son" (Matt. 11:27), and "No one can say Jesus is Lord except in the Holy Spirit" (1 Cor. 12:3).
>
> — ST. BASIL THE GREAT

God Is a Community of Persons

The Trinity is an essential theme for the apologist because it is the ultimate reality. It teaches us that to be perfect is to be self-gift. God is a triune community of perfectly self-giving Persons because God is love and, as Augustine once exclaimed so brilliantly, "Oh but you do see a trinity if you see charity." Wherever there is love, there is three—the lover, the Beloved, and the love who unites them. The principle of the universe, the ground of all being, is not the faceless concept of existence or shapeless cosmic power but Persons in a community of love.

This theological synthesis helped Christians through the centuries understand and clarify our theology of the Trinity. It is of course only with the revelation of Jesus Christ that we come to learn that "God is love"—a teaching found *only* in the Christian scriptures (1 John 4:8, 16). God is of course loving throughout the Old Testament, but he is never *named* "love." The ninety-nine names for God in Islam does not include "love." It is only with the advent of Jesus Christ that we learn God's ultimate identity as "Father" who eternally begets a "Son" in the "Holy Spirit."

This is who God ultimately is: three loving and beloved Persons sharing one divine nature. Imagine this perfect interrelationship every time you make the sign of the cross. We often do it so easily, even mindlessly, but crossing ourselves should be nothing less than a reaffirmation of the Trinity's indwelling in our life.

THE *TRISAGION*

✠ Holy God, Holy Mighty One, Holy Immortal One, have mercy on us.

Holy God, Holy Mighty One, Holy Immortal One, have mercy on us.

Holy God, Holy Mighty One, Holy Immortal One, have mercy on us.

Not all theists, of course, have been open to this gift of revelation. *Deists* over the centuries rejected any sort of personalization of the Godhead, notoriously reducing God to an "intelligent watchmaker." Mormons, Jehovah's Witnesses, Oneness Pentecostals, Unitarians, and other quasi-Christian groups substitute their own eccentric or reductionist theologies for the traditional Christian confession of the Trinity.

But the Bible never struggles to keep the oneness of God alongside his three-ness, mysterious though this is.

This is how traditional biblical interpretation understood God's declaration in Genesis, "*Let us* make human beings in *our* image, after *our* likeness" (Gen. 1:26a). We may also see this truth embedded in how Abraham addresses his three mysterious visitors in the singular (Gen. 18:1–3). What does King David mean when he says, "The Lord says to my lord: 'Sit at my right hand, while I make your enemies your footstool'" (Ps. 110:1) if not to foreshadow the Father's sending of the Son into the world to defeat the enemies of death and damnation?

The New Testament is of course even clearer: along with the Father, Jesus is God (John 8:58, 10:38, 14:10; Col. 2:9) and the Holy Spirit is God (Acts 5:3–4, 28:25–28; 1 Cor. 2:10–13). In the dynamic of love, the Son and the Spirit work always in tandem, one sending and the other sent: "When the Advocate comes whom I will send you from the Father, the Spirit of truth that proceeds from the Father, he will testify to me. And you also testify, because you have been with me from the beginning" (John 15:26–27).

> It is the Father who is the absolute principle in trinitarian life, the one who has no origin and from whom the divine life flows . . . "It is the Father who generates, the Son who is begotten, and the Holy Spirit who proceeds." The apostle John offers us a key to this mystery which infinitely surpasses our understanding, when in his first Letter he proclaims: "God is love" (1 John 4:8). This summit of revelation indicates that God is agape, that is, the gratuitous and total gift of self which Christ proved to us, especially by his death on the cross. The Father's infinite love for the world is revealed in Christ's sacrifice (cf. John 3:16; Rom. 5:8). The capacity to love infinitely, to give oneself without reserve or measure, belongs to God. By virtue of his being love, even before his free creation of the world he is Father in the divine life itself: a loving Father who generates the beloved Son and gives rise with him to the Holy Spirit, the Person—love, the reciprocal bond of communion.
>
> — POPE ST. JOHN PAUL II

God thus introduces the Trinity slowly, only after having revealed and well established his oneness. It would take the Church a few centuries more to clarify and formulate the truth of "one nature, three Persons" through the work of the

Cappadocian Fathers and the creeds and workings of the Councils of Nicaea (325) and I Constantinople (381).

TRINITARIAN SELECTION FROM THE NICENE CREED

✠ I believe in one God, the Father almighty, maker of heaven and earth, of all things visible and invisible.

I believe in one Lord Jesus Christ, the only begotten Son of God, born of the Father before all ages. God from God, light from light, true God from true God, begotten, not made, consubstantial with the Father; through him all things were made . . .

I believe in the Holy Spirit, the Lord, the giver of life, who proceeds from the Father and the Son, who with the Father and the Son is adored and glorified, who has spoken through the prophets.

If it weren't for the Trinity, how could we ever invoke God as Father? Of what or of whom would he *be* a Father? Who was he and what did he do for all eternity before he became *our* Father?

No, there can be no eternal Father without an eternal Son. When we think of the Trinity, we have to let go of the usual images of a human father who exists well before he begets a child in time. The three divine Persons of the Trinity do not come in or out of existence. One is not prior to any other: all are eternally, at once, who they always are. That is why Christians

God Is a Community of Persons

profess in the Nicene creed on Sundays that the Son is "eternally begotten"—meaning that there was never a time when the Father was not the Father, because the Son always is. In this eternal begetting, this timeless generation, the Spirit is the binding love, no less a Person, uniting the Father and Son together in a community of charity. The only "difference" (to use the word rhetorically) between the three is who each is before the other: the Father Begetter, the Son Begotten, and the Spirit the Gift between that Giver and Receiver.

> The divine Persons are relative to one another. Because it does not divide the divine unity, the real distinction of the Persons from one another resides solely in the relationships which relate them to one another: "In the relational names of the Persons the Father is related to the Son, the Son to the Father, and the Holy Spirit to both. While they are called three Persons in view of their relations, we believe in one nature or substance" (Council of Toledo, 589). Indeed "everything (in them) is one where there is no opposition of relationship" (Council of Florence, 1431–49). "Because of that unity the Father is wholly in the Son and wholly in the Holy Spirit; the Son is wholly in the Father and wholly in the Holy Spirit; the Holy Spirit is wholly in the Father and wholly in the Son" (Council of Florence).
>
> — *CATECHISM OF THE CATHOLIC CHURCH*

Here a beautiful truth merits our prayerful attention. Unlike us humans who have a core identity before and outside of any relationship—a man remains who he is whether he becomes "husband" or "father" or not, for example—it is not that way in the Godhead. God the Father is who he is as Father only because of the Son; the Son is who he is as Son only because he is begotten; the Holy Spirit is who he is as love because of the Father and Son's mutual union.

Dwell on that: the Persons of the Trinity are more reliant on each other than you and I are on one another! If someone's earthly child or parent dies, he remains who he is; yet it is not that way with God. This teaches us—and Christ embodies it perfectly in his incarnation and especially in his crucifixion—that intimacy, vulnerability, other-centeredness, and mutual reliance are not signs of weakness but are actually *divine attributes*.

> To love at all is to be vulnerable. Love anything, and your heart will certainly be wrung and possibly be broken. If you want to make sure of keeping it intact, you must give it to no one and nothing, not even an animal. You must carefully wrap it round with hobbies and little luxuries and routine and avoidances of entanglement, and then lock it up in the casket or coffin of your own selfishness. And this means that in the long run, the alternative to tragedy, or at least to the threat of tragedy, is damnation, for in that casket—safe, still, and unventilated in the darkness—it

God Is a Community of Persons

will go bad; not broken, but finally unbreakable,
impenetrable, resistant to all good and joy.

— C.S. LEWIS

It can be illuminating to realize that the Latin term for "wound" is *vulnera*—thus, vulnerability literally means *the ability to be wounded*. To open our hearts to another, even to Perfect Love himself, means to risk a life outside of ourselves. This is what it means to be made for communion, to find our truest self in the life of another. This is what the Trinity has modeled from all time, and this is what we too must become if we ever want to experience the fullness of what it means to be a person, what it means to be human.

> I confess and do not deny that you loved me before
> I existed, and that your love for me is ineffable,
> as if you were mad with love for your creature.
>
> O, eternal Trinity! oh Godhead! which Godhead
> gave value to the blood of your Son, you, oh
> eternal Trinity, are a deep sea, into which the
> deeper I enter the more I find, and the more I
> find the more I seek; the soul cannot be satiated
> in your abyss, for she continually hungers after
> you, the eternal Trinity, desiring to see you with
> light in your light. As the heart desires the spring
> of living water, so my soul desires to leave the
> prison of this dark body and see you in truth.

How long, O eternal Trinity, fire and abyss of love, will your face be hidden from my eyes? Melt at once the cloud of my body. The knowledge that you have given me of yourself in your truth constrains me to long to abandon the heaviness of my body, and to give my life for the glory and praise of your name. For I have tasted and seen with the light of the intellect in your light, the abyss of you—the eternal Trinity, and the beauty of your creature, for, looking at myself in you, I saw myself to be your image, my life being given me by your power, O eternal Father; and your wisdom, which belongs to your only begotten Son, shining in my intellect and my will, being one with your Holy Spirit, who proceeds from you and your Son, by whom I am able to love you.

— ST. CATHERINE OF SIENA

As we approached the unapproachable God, we had to pass through his Ten Commandments. We examined our conscience to unearth ways we have said "no" to God. This is a practice that should be done often, certainly weekly, if not daily! To know our sins is not easy and to name them is even more difficult, so it takes constant practice. It also requires the cultivation of humility and self-knowledge to be able not only to say, "I have greatly sinned" but "here is how and why."

To go even deeper, St. Ignatius of Loyola (1491–1556) devised a way of examining our soul that moved away from

An Examination of Consciousness

looking only at the sinful thoughts, words, and deeds of our day. Ignatius's introspection begins not with sins but with gratitude and the cataloging of daily blessings. This manner of praying later came to be called an *Examination of Consciousness*, to distinguish it from what was done before the sacrament of reconciliation. A different contour arises in our souls when we look primarily at the concrete ways God has been blessing us. We thank him for waking up, for those at home, for our work, for the sunshine and the rain; we thank him for our vigor and health, for our children's safe arrival to school, for hot water and electricity in our homes accomplishes for us, for food and drink, and all the myriad ways that our heavenly Father takes care of us.

You can think of the Examination of Consciousness in five steps:

1. Intentionally call to mind the awareness that you are in God's presence, and that he loves you as much right now in this moment than ever before. You are loved. You are blessed. Ask now for an increase of awareness and gratitude for all the gifts God gives you.

   Lord, you created me out of love for me and now call me to participate in all the graces you have in store for me, transforming me daily into a greater lover and friend.

2. Bring to mind the past twenty-hour hours. Review all the emotions and encounters you experienced. Be very concrete, trying to recall how you felt when this or that just happened to work out for you, or how you might have taken for granted this or that daily blessing, or what emotions welled up in you when you

saw this person or found yourself in this particular place, and so on.

Lord, I can grow so entitled in all the blessings I have come to expect and sometimes think I have learned. Soften my heart and illumine my mind to see all things in my life as your gift to me.

3. Now, speak to God as a friend by choosing one or two experiences that stand out to you more than others. Perhaps it was a conversation you had with a loved one; perhaps it was a moment of reconciliation with someone with whom you had a tense moment; perhaps it was a chance encounter with a stranger. Here, beg God to see him more alive and active in your daily experiences and in all the *benefits of being you* that you enjoy. Stay here, offering Jesus whatever emotions arise—perhaps it is gratitude, but maybe it is stress or unexplained anxiety.

   Jesus, help me see why I am feeling this way.

4. Obviously, no day passes without some disappointment. Pick one sin and ask forgiveness for it. Ask God to help you see why you did it. Tell him whatever it is you need to say here, being not only contrite but concrete. Does any pattern of sinfulness emerge?

   Jesus, you died for my sins. Increase my sorrow I allow you to die for me. The needs I feel overwhelm me and I can take my frustration out on your other sons and daughters. Forgive me and grant me the grace to remain always in your peace and in the security of your love.

An Examination of Consciousness

5. Bring to prayer the *next* twenty-four hours. What faces you tomorrow? Whom will you meet and what might be said? Place yourself in any upcoming situation you might find important and ask the Holy Spirit to guide your words and actions and entire demeanor in this encounter. If you use a calendar or planner, you can include it in your prayer, perhaps putting your hand over the list of meetings and agenda of things to get done, asking God to make the next day as holy as possible.

Master of my life and myself, be with me as this night descends and as a new day unfolds. Guide me the gifts of trust and confidence, that you are ever at work in me and this entire universe has been created for me to find my salvation and to glorify your holy name.

St. Ignatius then suggests ending with an Our Father or Hail Mary.
Obviously, some days nothing will really stand out to you. Be patient with yourself and simply sit with what might come to mind. If nothing, stay quiet for the allotted time you reserved for this daily exercise. Is this a pattern? Do you feel anxiously empty or just peacefully still before your own life? Are there past hurts that need to be addressed before you can grow in gratitude? Are there perhaps amends you must make with another before you can truly open your heart up to God?

TO THE HOLY SPIRIT

✠ Glory to thee, O Lord, glory to thee!

O heavenly king, the Comforter, the Spirit of truth
who art everywhere and fill all things,
the treasury of blessings and the giver of life,
come and abide in us, and cleanse us from every
impurity, and save our souls, O Good One.

Holy God, Holy Mighty, Holy Immortal,
Have mercy on us.

2

God's Good Creation

When I see your heavens, the work of
your fingers,
the moon and stars that you set in place—
What is man that you are mindful of him,
and a son of man that you care for him?
Yet you have made him little less than a god,
crowned him with glory and honor.
You have given him rule over the works
of your hands,
put all things at his feet:
All sheep and oxen, even the beasts of the field,
The birds of the air, the fish of the sea,
and whatever swims the paths of the seas.
O Lord, our Lord,
how awesome is your name through all the earth!

— PSALM 8:4–10

THE SOUL OF APOLOGETICS

When we engage in apologetics or evangelization, often the topic moves from God himself to what God has made. How could God create out of nothing? How can creation be good? How can a good God allow such terrible evils in the supposedly good world he made? What does it mean to be human?

Of course, the Christian answers to these fundamental questions are coherent, plausible, and positive. Yet in a world shot through with such skepticism, cynicism, and suffering we must work to prepare ourselves not just intellectually but spiritually to present those answers in a way that communicates the sovereignty of God, the goodness of all creation, and the dignity and freedom of the human race.

> The main point of Christianity was this: that nature is not our mother: Nature is our sister. We can be proud of her beauty, since we have the same father; but she has no authority over us; we have to admire, but not to imitate. This gives to the typically Christian pleasure in this earth a strange touch of lightness that is almost frivolity. Nature was a solemn mother to the worshipers of Isis and Cybele. Nature was a solemn mother to Wordsworth or to Emerson. But nature is not solemn to Francis of Assisi or to George Herbert. To St. Francis, nature is a sister, and even a younger sister: a little, dancing sister, to be laughed at as well as loved.
>
> — G.K. CHESTERTON

How might we laugh and love with creation, without ever being beholden to it—or worse, worshiping it? We can do so by only approaching this world as God's first gift to those made in his image and likeness. Creation is his; yet he has gifted its stewardship to us, those for whom he created it in the first place.

> Our God, God of all men
> God of heaven and earth, seas and rivers,
> God of sun and moon, of all the stars,
> God of high mountain and lowly valley,
> God over heaven, and in heaven, and under heaven.
> He has a dwelling in heaven and earth and sea
> and in all things that are in them.
> He inspires all things, he quickens all things.
> He is over all things, he supports all things.
> He makes the light of the sun to shine,
> He surrounds the moon and the stars,
> He has made wells in the arid earth,
> Placed dry islands in the sea.
> He has a Son co-eternal with himself . . .
> And the Holy Spirit breathes in them;
> Not separate are the Father and the
> Son and the Holy Spirit.
>
> — ATTRIBUTED TO ST. PATRICK

God creates, we believe, *ex caritate*—out of love.

If we recall our image of Christianity as a reflection of the human heart, we can ask: what is the first thing love longs to do? What is the first impulse of a lover toward his or her beloved? Is it not the bestowal of gifts? We long to be good to those we love; we look for ways to provide for them, and traditionally such benevolence is the first characteristic of charity. This is how to understand God's original act outside of himself. Creation is the *primal gift of God to the human race*.

Benevolence is the first sign of love because love naturally desires that one's beloved have the best of gifts. Have you ever wondered why a perfectly sufficient being would freely choose to bring out of nothing an entire world well below himself? God's acting solely on our behalf is an unparalleled act of generosity: here there is absolutely no trace of debt or a gift given in hope of a better one being given in return. The Godhead chooses to create solely out of love, knowing that the height of this gift—the human person—would enjoy being alive in a universe teeming with creatures of all sorts, with hundreds of billions of galaxies, brimming with colors and hues and textures, with angels whose celestial existence bring unhidden joys, and a human race whom he formed—and will save—out of nothing other than love.

What does an authentic Catholic theology of creation entail? First and foremost, we must rediscover a childlike wonder before all the manifestations of God's love for us. That is what creation is: a reflection of the Trinity's own love. Before talk of the earth and of "ecology" became politicized, the great saints were able to offer counsel for Christians to become more aware of God's presence in and through all that he creates.

> Therefore, whoever is not illumined by such great splendors in created things is blind. Anyone who is not awakened by such great outcries is deaf. Anyone who is not led from such great effects to

God's Good Gift to Us

> give praise to God is mute. Anyone who does not turn to the first Principle as a result of such signs is a fool. Therefore, open your eyes, alert your spiritual ears, unlock your lips and apply your heart, so that in all the creatures, you may see, hear, praise, love and adore, magnify and honor God, lest the entire world rise up against you.
>
> — ST. BONAVENTURE

Is love a sufficient enough answer to explain God's choosing to create a cosmos that he in no way needs? It is if we are clear that the love he longs to create is not his but *ours*. Perhaps no one understood this dynamic of divine love in and through creation as well as the great poet Dante Alighieri (1265–1321). The Florentine bard understood well how creation adds nothing to God's love, but instead allows for us creatures to experience new loves, which pleases the eternal Lover.

> Not to increase Its good—no mil nor dram
> can add to true perfection, but that reflections
> of his reflection might declare "I am"—
> in his eternity; beyond time, above
> all other comprehension, as it pleased him
> new loves were born of the Eternal Love.
>
> — DANTE

Are you free enough to encounter everyone you meet as a "reflection of his reflection"? For every human person is an image and a likeness of God himself. All persons, all things, exist because God is love; and out of love and for love he brings all into being. Such a claim, though audacious, is not difficult to imagine when we think of how human couples do not ask their children if they wish to be conceived, born, and nurtured. We may likewise present creation as God's knowing well beforehand that the human race would enjoy existing, living with reason and community, surrounded by all the material as well as spiritual goods and blessings only God can bring about. This is the first movement of love: the benevolent bestowal of good gifts for the sake of the beloved.

> Bless the Lord, my soul!
> Lord, my God, you are great indeed!
> You are clothed with majesty and splendor, robed in light as with a cloak.
> You spread out the heavens like a tent;
> setting the beams of your chambers upon the waters.
> You make the clouds your chariot; traveling on
> the wings of the wind.
> You make the winds your messengers; flaming fire, your ministers.
> You fixed the earth on its foundation, so it
> can never be shaken.
> The deeps covered it like a garment; above the mountains stood the waters.
> At your rebuke they took flight; at the sound of your thunder they fled.
> They rushed up the mountains, down the valleys to the place you had fixed for them.

God's Good Gift to Us

You set a limit they cannot pass; never again will
they cover the earth.
You made springs flow in wadies that wind
among the mountains.
They give drink to every beast of the field; here wild
asses quench their thirst.
Beside them the birds of heaven nest; among
the branches they sing.
You water the mountains from your chambers;
from the fruit of your labor the earth abounds.
You make the grass grow for the cattle and
plants for people's work
to bring forth food from the earth, wine to
gladden their hearts,
oil to make their faces shine, and bread to
sustain the human heart.
The trees of the Lord drink their fill, the cedars of
Lebanon, which you planted.
There the birds build their nests; the stork in the
junipers, its home.
The high mountains are for wild goats; the rocky
cliffs, a refuge for badgers.
You made the moon to mark the seasons, the sun
that knows the hour of its setting.
You bring darkness and night falls, then all the
animals of the forest wander about.
Young lions roar for prey; they seek
their food from God.
When the sun rises, they steal away and

> settle down in their dens.
> People go out to their work, to their
> labor till evening falls.
> How varied are your works, Lord!
> In wisdom you have made them all; the earth is
> full of your creatures.
> Bless the Lord, my soul! Hallelujah!
>
> — PSALM 104:1–24, 35

St. Augustine argued that the first gift God created for this world was the angels. Since the physical lights of the universe do not appear until God creates them on the fourth day (Gen. 1:14), how should we make sense of the "light" that God speaks into being on the first day? For Augustine, this light refers to the angels who were originally created totally in God's refulgence.

Reflecting God's own brilliance, the angels were brought about to live face to face with God but, as the story unfolds, some turned away from God and sank miserably into their own pride. This is why God did not "create" dark but simply separated those fallen lights (angels) from those who remained eternally steadfast: "God saw that the light was good. God then separated the light from the darkness" (Gen. 1:4).

Angels appear all throughout the rest of the Old Testament as well: they are sent before the patriarchs to lead them safely on their exodus (Exod. 23:20–21), they lead God's armies in battles (Jos. 5:13–15), they comfort and strengthen those who are weakening (Judg. 6:11–24); and even mighty Raphael, who is "one of the seven angels who stand and serve before the glory of the Lord" (Tob. 12:15), is sent to assist a newly married couple in their service to God and neighbor.

The Angels: Messengers of God's Ways

Of course Jesus himself confirms the existence of angels, teaching us in fact that every human being has been assigned a personal angelic intercessor in heaven whose entire existence, it seems, is to guard those to whom they have been assigned on earth: "See that you do not despise one of these little ones, for I say to you that their angels in heaven always look upon the face of my heavenly Father" (Matt. 18:10).

If the Bible does not convince, philosophers too have deduced the existence of angels. How so? Think how angels fill what would otherwise be a metaphysical gap in the cosmos. There are three types of persons: divine, angelic, and human. The three divine Persons of the Trinity are uncreated and pure spirit, whereas humans are created with spirits and bodies. Is it therefore not reasonable to think that in the middle of these two classifications there are persons who are created spiritual substances—spirit but no body?

PADRE PIO'S PRAYER TO HIS GUARDIAN ANGEL

✠ Oh, my holy guardian angel, care for
my soul and my body.
Enlighten my mind that I may better
know the Lord my God
and love him with all my heart.
Watch over me when I pray so I won't give into
life's distractions.
Sustain me with your counsel as I live as a
righteous Christian,
and help me to do good works with a giving heart.

THE SOUL OF APOLOGETICS

Protect me from the cunning of the adversary, and lift me up when I am being tempted so I may win the fight against evil. Stay beside me at all times, never stop watching over me until I'm called back to the father's house, where we will praise together our great God for all eternity.

After celebrating Mass early one morning in 1884, Pope Leo XIII collapsed and almost died. When he was brought to, he reported having witnessed the devil devouring souls, particularly throughout the twenty-first century. In this vision, Leo saw St. Michael the Archangel confront Satan and defeat him in battle, leading the pope to compose this prayer and entrust it to the Church, traditionally said immediately after the celebration of Mass.

ST. MICHAEL PRAYER (restored translation)

✠ St. Michael the Archangel, defend us in battle.
Be our protection against the wickedness and snares of the devil.
May God rebuke him, we humbly pray.
And do thou, O Prince of the heavenly host,
by the power of God,
bind Satan and all the evil spirits who prowl about

The Angels: Messengers of God's Ways

the world seeking the ruin of souls, and thrust them into hell.

It is important to recognize that the heavenly realm was brought into existence not only for God's greater glory but to *assist in the workings of this world*. In fact, the Greek-derived word *angel* literally means "messenger," signaling that angels have been created to bring God's words and ways to the human race.

This ordering of creatures points to nothing other than the Church, a gathering of all God's gifts. It is an ancient and consistent teaching, then, that the universe was brought into existence for the glorification of humanity, united in the Church.

> Christians of the first centuries said, "The world was created for the sake of the Church" (Shepherd of Hermas, Vision 2.4.1). God created the world for the sake of communion with his divine life, a communion brought about by the "convocation" of men in Christ, and this "convocation" is the Church. The Church is the goal of all things (St. Epiphanius, Panarion 1,1,5), and God permitted such painful upheavals as the angels' fall and man's sin only as occasions and means for displaying all the power of his arm and the whole measure of the love he wanted to give the world: "Just as God's will is creation and is called 'the world,' so his intention is the salvation of men, and it is called 'the Church.'"
>
> — *CATECHISM OF THE CATHOLIC CHURCH*

THE SOUL OF APOLOGETICS

Even if humanity had not sinned, the purpose of our creation would be the same: our eternal and perfectly joyful union with God. This union is never singular but always communal, the convocation—or "calling together"—of God's family, the Church.

This is a Church that in a sense begins with the creation of the angels and is threaded through every single living creature. This is how the heavens and the earth can proclaim God's glory: by being receptive to the existence he gives each things. It is not incidental that the end time is described in terms of a "new heaven and a new earth," as our present earth has a true and preliminary role to play in our eternal salvation.

> The heavens declare the glory of God; the
> firmament proclaims the works of his hands.
>
> Day unto day pours forth speech; night
> unto night whispers knowledge.
>
> There is no speech, no words;
> their voice is not heard;
>
> A report goes forth through all the earth,
> their messages, to the ends of the world.
>
> He has pitched in them a tent for the sun; it
> comes forth like a bridegroom from his canopy,
> and like a hero joyfully runs its course.

The Angels: Messengers of God's Ways

From one end of the heavens it comes
forth; its course runs through to the
other; nothing escapes its heat.

— PSALM 19:2–7

God's creating *ex caritate* is also his creating *ex nihilo*—God creates out of love by creating out of nothing. He simply speaks, and things come to be that were not.

For he spoke, and it came to be,
commanded, and it stood in place.

— PSALM 33:9

Let your every creature serve you; for you spoke,
and they were made. You sent forth your Spirit,
and it created them; no one can resist your voice.

— JUDITH 16:14

Look at the heavens and the earth and see all
that is in them; then you will know that God
did not make them out of existing things.

— 2 MACCABEES 7:28

As it is written, 'I have made you father of many
nations.' He is our father in the sight of God, in

whom he believed, who gives life to the dead and calls into being what does not exist.

— ROMANS 4:17

In the early centuries of the Church, Christians were forced to defend this position against pagan creation myths that assumed that God simply wrestled into order pre-existing cosmic matter. The Babylonians, for example, had imagined that the physical world as we now know it came to be through the bloody battles of warring gods. Greek philosophy, on the other hand, posited a world in which pre-existing matter is wrought into physical things by a "demiurge" that seeks, imperfectly, to make tangible the perfect world of immaterial forms.

We believe that God needs no pre-existent thing or any help in order to create, nor is creation any sort of necessary emanation from the divine substance. God creates freely "out of nothing": "If God had drawn the world from pre-existent matter, what would be so extraordinary in that? A human artisan makes from a given material whatever he wants, while God shows his power by starting from nothing to make all he wants."

— ST. THEOPHILUS OF ANTIOCH

A World Brought Out of Nothing by Love

ANCIENT LATIN PRAYER AT THE ORATE, FRATRES

✠ The creature can offer nothing to the Creator that can be worthy of his acceptance; I unite myself, therefore, to the sacrifice of Jesus Christ, which can alone merit anything in my behalf.

I desire nothing but through him and with him. I have no wish but to belong to him. O God of mercy, I seek nothing but thy love.

Graciously accept the sacrifice of my heart and of my whole self, and may it, like the sacrifice of Jesus, be pleasing to thee and unite us to him.

Both of these creation stories assume that matter is both eternal and by nature unwieldy and disordered. The deity in charge is forced to grapple with this cosmic enemy either by way of hostile force or philosophical reasoning. But Genesis blows up both those fantastical ancient myths and philosophical theories, presenting an unparalleled image of a deity who creates simply by commanding it. How differently our faith understands the first moment of creation and thus the God who creates and the world he created! Our loving God freely and joyfully brings a world out of nothing, says that it is *good*, and presents it to his beloved sons and daughters.

> Since God could create everything out of nothing, he can also, through the Holy Spirit, give spiritual

life to sinners by creating a pure heart in them, (cf. Ps. 51:12) and bodily life to the dead through the Resurrection. God "gives life to the dead and calls into existence the things that do not exist" (cf. Rom. 4:17). And since God was able to make light shine in darkness by his Word, he can also give the light of faith to those who do not yet know him (cf. Gen. 1:3; 1 Cor. 4:6).

— CATECHISM OF THE CATHOLIC CHURCH

Sacred Scripture opens by attesting to how all things came into being simply by divine decree. There was no pre-existing matter, and no rival to God—nothing apart from the Father, the Son, and the Holy Spirit. But at one eternal moment, the Holy Trinity chose to create time and space and all that fills it. God alone can do this. It is true power. It is true love.

How differently we humans must act! We can only "make" or "generate" things from pre-existing matter. We make chairs out of the wood provided by a forest, clothing by the fabric made from wool and cotton; but technically we never "create," because creation is taking something out of nothing. Even our ideas, even our songs and our novels, are fashioned from things our senses have taken in and our intellects have synthesized.

What above all characterizes this creation God has brought about from nothing? Its goodness! Read the first chapter of Genesis, very slowly, and notice the litany running through it: "and God saw that it was good." It ends with an even greater exclamation, at the end of the six days of creation: "God looked at everything he had made, and found it *very good*" (Gen. 1:31).

A World Brought Out of Nothing by Love

All things are good because all things come from and are sustained in existence by God, the one being who can bring about all that is. As a community of love, the Trinity wanted to share this love with others, so he created a world in which for other persons to live and to flourish. This is the beginning of our human history: that from love we have come, by love we are to live, and toward love we are all ordered.

PRAYER OF DANIEL
(Dan. 2:20–23)

☧ Blessed be the name of God forever and ever, for wisdom and power are his.

He causes the changes of the times and seasons, establishes kings and deposes them.

He gives wisdom to the wise and knowledge to those who understand.

He reveals deep and hidden things and knows what is in the darkness, for the light dwells with him.

To you, God of my ancestors, I give thanks and praise, because you have given me wisdom and power. Now you have shown me what we asked of you, you have made known to us the king's dream.

THE SOUL OF APOLOGETICS

Among many gifts of wisdom that Daniel received from the Lord may have been his poetic awareness of how all things praise God simply by *being what they are*. God's first gift to every creature is the essence of what it is; and all of them together, just by being, form a harmonious chorus of praise. All things give glory to God by fulfilling their nature. This is how Daniel can be so lyrical in seeing how all things shout praise to God by being naturally what they are. Having been created out of nothing, all creatures wear this badge of gratitude, thanking the Lord for having brought them about.

> Bless the Lord, all you works of the Lord,
> praise and exalt him above all forever.
>
> Angels of the Lord, bless the Lord,
> praise and exalt him above all forever.
>
> You heavens, bless the Lord,
> praise and exalt him above all forever.
>
> All you waters above the heavens, bless the Lord,
> praise and exalt him above all forever.
>
> All you powers, bless the Lord;
> praise and exalt him above all forever.
>
> Sun and moon, bless the Lord;
> praise and exalt him above all forever.
>
> Stars of heaven, bless the Lord;
> praise and exalt him above all forever.
>
> Every shower and dew, bless the Lord;
> praise and exalt him above all forever.
>
> All you winds, bless the Lord;
> praise and exalt him above all forever.

All Things Glorify God in Their Nature

Fire and heat, bless the Lord;
praise and exalt him above all forever.

Cold and chill, bless the Lord;
praise and exalt him above all forever.

Dew and rain, bless the Lord;
praise and exalt him above all forever.

Frost and chill, bless the Lord;
praise and exalt him above all forever.

Hoarfrost and snow, bless the Lord;
praise and exalt him above all forever.

Nights and days, bless the Lord;
praise and exalt him above all forever.

Light and darkness, bless the Lord;
praise and exalt him above all forever.

Lightnings and clouds, bless the Lord;
praise and exalt him above all forever.

Let the earth bless the Lord,
praise and exalt him above all forever.

Mountains and hills, bless the Lord;
praise and exalt him above all forever.

Everything growing on earth, bless the Lord;
praise and exalt him above all forever.

You springs, bless the Lord;
praise and exalt him above all forever.

Seas and rivers, bless the Lord;
praise and exalt him above all forever.

You sea monsters and all water creatures, bless the Lord;
praise and exalt him above all forever.

THE SOUL OF APOLOGETICS

> All you birds of the air, bless the Lord;
> praise and exalt him above all forever.
>
> All you beasts, wild and tame, bless the Lord;
> praise and exalt him above all forever.
>
> All you mortals, bless the Lord;
> praise and exalt him above all forever.
>
> O Israel, bless the Lord;
> praise and exalt him above all forever.
>
> Priests of the Lord, bless the Lord;
> praise and exalt him above all forever.
>
> Servants of the Lord, bless the Lord;
> praise and exalt him above all forever.
>
> Spirits and souls of the just, bless the Lord;
> praise and exalt him above all forever.
>
> Holy and humble of heart, bless the Lord;
> praise and exalt him above all forever.
>
> — DANIEL 3:57–87

Having this awareness is not, of course, to place inanimate and subhuman creatures on par with persons who can glorify God freely, infinitely, actively, and consciously. But it is a way to re-discover our Catholic tradition's rich appreciation for how all creation, as fallen and disrupted it may seem at times, is truly the Lord's gift to us.

> Prayer is the wall of faith: her arms and missiles
> against the foe who keeps watch over us on all
> sides. And, so never walk we unarmed. By day, be

All Things Glorify God in Their Nature

we mindful of Station; by night, of vigil. Under the arms of prayer guard we the standard of our General; await we in prayer the angel's trump. The angels, likewise, all pray; every creature prays; cattle and wild beasts pray and bend their knees; and when they issue from their layers and lairs, they look up heavenward with no idle mouth, making their breath vibrate after their own manner. Nay, the birds too, rising out of the nest, upraise themselves heavenward, and, instead of hands, expand the cross of their wings, and say somewhat to seem like prayer. What more then, touching the office of prayer? Even the Lord himself prayed; to whom be honor and virtue unto the ages of the ages!

— TERTULLIAN

When we can allow ourselves to see the world with such childlike wonder, nature is neither a goddess demanding our devotion nor a morally voided wasteland good only for exploitation.

Did not Jesus walk this earth in a manner that saw not only other persons but all creatures differently? Does he not give us the mandate to "go into the whole world and proclaim the gospel to *every creature*" (Mark 16:15)? St. Paul, too, instructs us not to turn away "from the hope of the gospel that you have heard, which has been preached to every creature under heaven" (Col. 1:23). What might this mean?

When asked what constitutes a truly Christian heart, a merciful heart, the seventh-century ascetic Isaac of Nineveh saw how all of creation groans for greater fulfillment in the

Lord (Rom. 8:22). Accordingly, the Christian offers prayers and praise for all creation.

> And, so, when asked: "And what is a merciful heart?" He replied, "The heart's burning for all creation, for human beings, for birds and animals, and for demons, and everything there is. At the recollection of them and at the sight of them his eyes gush forth with tears owing to the force of the compassion which constrains his heart, so that, as a result of its abundant sense of mercy, the heart shrinks and cannot bear to hear or examine any harm or small suffering of anything in creation. For this reason he offers up prayer with tears at all times, even for irrational animals, and for the enemies of truth, and for those who harm him, for their preservation and being forgiven. As a result of the immense compassion infused in his heart without measure—like God's—he even does this for reptiles."
>
> — ISAAC OF NINEVEH

Knowing that "in God's hands is the soul of every living thing" (Job 12:10), some saints have actually preached to lower creatures—only not for the "salvation" of animal souls but for their own. How so? To have dominion is also to *domesticate*: to use our personhood to elevate creation to a higher level. As we train an otherwise feral animal to know the ways and workings of our home, God brings us into his own divine personhood and elevates us into his ways and workings. We can teach a dog,

All Things Glorify God in Their Nature

for example, to be somewhat like a family member—knowing where to go, what to eat, and so on; similarly, in his Church, God makes us one of his own, teaching us how to act like one of his own children. This is what it means to share the divine life (2 Pet. 1:4), and perhaps God has given us the goodness of creation to let us enjoy a faint experience of what he longs for with us.

CANTICLE OF THE SUN

O most High, almighty, good Lord God,
to you belong praise, glory, honor, and all blessing!
Praised be my Lord God with all creatures;
and especially our brother the sun,
which brings us the day, and the light;
fair is he, and shining with a very great splendor:
O Lord, he signifies you to us!
Praised be my Lord for our sister the moon,
and for the stars, which God has set clear
and lovely in heaven.
Praised be my Lord for our brother the wind,
and for air and cloud, calms and all weather,
by which you uphold in life all creatures.
Praised be my Lord for our sister water,
which is very serviceable to us,
and humble, and precious, and clean.
Praised be my Lord for brother fire,
through which you give us light in the darkness:
and he is bright, and pleasant, and

very mighty, and strong.
Praised be my Lord for our mother the Earth,
which sustains us and keeps us,
and yields divers fruits, and flowers of
many colors, and grass.
Praised be my Lord for all those who pardon one
another for God's love's sake,
and who endure weakness and tribulation;
blessed are they who peaceably shall endure,
for you, O most High, shall give them a crown!
Praised be my Lord for our sister, the death of the
body, from which no one escapes.
Woe to him who dies in mortal sin!
Blessed are they who are found walking by
your most holy will,
for the second death shall have no
power to do them harm.
Praise you, and bless you the Lord, and
give thanks to God,
and serve God with great humility.

— ST. FRANCIS OF ASSISI

The Catholic mind has always equated being with goodness: the greater a being, the better the being. This means, first, that in God's good creation there are no intrinsically evil things. If something *is*, it is *good*. This includes even Satan and the worst of human sinners. No matter how much one of God's rational

The Order of Goodness in Creation

creatures misuses his will and gifts, in their existence they are still good. All beings and things thus have instilled in them a certain ineradicable dignity: from the smallest of subatomic particles to the loftiest (or lowest) of angels. Every person to whom we try to defend or explain the Faith, whether a goodwilled seeker or a vicious foe of Christ and his Church, falls somewhere in between! Let us imitate God and keep in mind their goodness at all times.

Since being and goodness are interchangeable, an obvious *order* of goodness becomes discernible in the cosmos. God's creation is hierarchically arranged, with God at the utmost top and the imperceptible components that make up material things at the bottom. This shows us a clear arrangement of the priorities we should have: with our obligations to God and created persons highest, and our attention to lower material goods far below.

Now we can see how, by viewing the universe not as a mishmash of random chaos but as an ordered series of good gifts reaching from the material to the spiritual, a *morality* begins to emerge. In fact, *only* such an ordered universe makes real morality possible.

> Goodness and being are really the same, and differ only in idea; which is clear from the following argument. The essence of goodness consists in this, that it is in some way desirable. Hence the Philosopher says, "Goodness is what all desire." Now it is clear that a thing is desirable only in so far as it is perfect; for all desire their own perfection. But everything is perfect so far as it is actual. Therefore it is clear that a thing is perfect

so far as it exists; for it is existence that makes all things actual, as is clear from the foregoing. Hence it is clear that goodness and being are the same really. But goodness presents the aspect of desirableness, which being does not present.

— ST. THOMAS AQUINAS

Yet, if all things are good, how do we explain the obvious problem of evil?

This is a key theme for any apologist, because it might be the number one reason (or excuse) people cite for not taking Christianity seriously: "How can a good God allow for so much suffering in this world?" This is called the question of *theodicy:* the quest to understand how we can reconcile a good God and the perception of evil all around us.

> If God the Father almighty, the Creator of the ordered and good world, cares for all his creatures, why does evil exist? To this question, as pressing as it is unavoidable and as painful as it is mysterious, no quick answer will suffice. Only Christian faith as a whole constitutes the answer to this question: the goodness of creation, the drama of sin and the patient love of God who comes to meet man by his covenants, the redemptive incarnation of his Son, his gift of the Spirit, his gathering of the Church, the power of the sacraments and his call to a blessed life to which free creatures are invited to consent in advance, but from which, by a terrible

The Order of Goodness in Creation

mystery, they can also turn away in advance. There is not a single aspect of the Christian message that is not in part an answer to the question of evil.

— CATECHISM OF THE CATHOLIC CHURCH

As Christianity emerged in the ancient world, certain heresies (known collectively today as *Gnosticism*) arose in an attempt to answer the problem of evil. For example, Manichaeism (founded in the third century by a Persian mystic Mani) held that since this world is obviously at war with itself—some things seem good and other things bad—there must be two gods: one good god of spirit and light and another malevolent god who reigns over the material and crass.

This idea was so alluring that even someone as bright as St. Augustine was in thrall to the Manichean sect for nine years. Even for Augustine, at least for a while, it seemed to make sense that the base and physical things of the world (giving rise to evil) could not have come from the same god who created wisdom and goodness.

Only after coming to the Catholic understanding of evil not as a thing that exists (because remember, being and goodness are interchangeable qualities) but as the *lack* of a good that *should* be in a thing (what he called a *privation*), could Augustine understand how all things do in fact come from the one good God—but that good things could nonetheless be agents or tools of evil acts.

In his commentary on Genesis aimed against his former sect, the Manicheans, Augustine compares them to men who walk into a master craftsman's workshop too ignorant to understand what all the tools and instruments are for. In the mind of the craftsman, though, everything has its own unique purpose and need.

> But when they say things like that, they are failing to understand how all these things are beautiful to their maker and craftsman, who has a use for them all in his management of the whole universe which is under control of his sovereign law. After all, if a layman enters a mechanic's workshop, he will see many instruments there whose purpose he is ignorant of, and of which, if he is more than usually silly, he thinks are superfluous. What's more, if he carelessly tumbles into the furnace, or cuts himself on a sharp steel implement when he handles it wrongly, then he reckons that there are many pernicious and harmful things there too. The mechanic, however, who knows the use of everything there, has a good laugh at his silliness, takes no notice of his inept remarks, and just presses on with the work in hand.
>
> — ST. AUGUSTINE

Would the modern Puritan not do well to pray over this passage? If a Bordeaux brings about drunkenness, that bottle of wine is being used wrongly. If a beautiful body elicits lust, the ogler is using his vision wrongly. If your neighbor's accomplishments bring about envy, you are looking upon success and human worth wrongly. There is no evil in a "thing," but only in

The Order of Goodness in Creation

the fallen will, in the desire that seeks its own immediate satisfaction over the way God himself has intended all things to be.

> Our body is a cenacle; a monstrance: through its crystal the world should see God.
>
> — ST. GIANNA MOLLA

PRAYER FOR DELIVERANCE FROM EVIL
Pope St. John Paul II

✠ Immaculate Heart! Help us to conquer
the menace of evil,
which so easily takes root in the hearts of
the people of today,
and whose immeasurable effects already weigh down
upon our modern world
and seem to block the paths toward the future!

From famine and war, deliver us.
From nuclear war, from incalculable self-destruction,
from every kind of war, deliver us.
From sins against the life of man from its very
beginning, deliver us.
From hatred and from the demeaning of the dignity
of the children of God, deliver us.

From every kind of injustice in the life of society, deliver us.
From readiness to trample on the commandments of God, deliver us.
From attempts to stifle in human hearts the very truth of God, deliver us.
From the loss of awareness of good and evil, deliver us.
From sins against the Holy Spirit, deliver us, deliver us.

Accept, O Mother of Christ, this cry laden with the sufferings
of all individual human beings, laden with the sufferings of whole societies.
Help us with the power of the Holy Spirit to conquer all sin:
individual sin and the "sin of the world," sin in all its manifestations.
Let there be revealed, once more, in the history of the world
the infinite saving power of the Redemption: the power of merciful love!
May it put a stop to evil!
May it transform consciences!

Types and Grades of Sin

May your Immaculate Heart reveal for
all the light of hope!

THE JESUS PRAYER

✠ Lord Jesus, Son of God,
have mercy on me, a sinner.

When the order of creation is inverted, evils arise. The apostle John tells us that there are two kinds of sins: the kind that is deadly (*mortal*) and cannot just be prayed away, and another kind that is not deadly, which he does not name but which Tradition has called *venial*.

> If anyone sees his brother sinning, if the sin is
> not deadly, he should pray to God and he will
> give him life. This is only for those whose sin is
> not deadly. There is such a thing as deadly sin,
> about which I do not say that you should pray. All
> wrongdoing is sin, but there is sin that is not deadly.
>
> — 1 JOHN 5:16–17

In the early third century, Tertullian numbered the "deadly sins" at seven, and a century or so later, they were listed in order by a Greek-speaking monk named Evagrius of Pontus:

- Pride
- Envy
- Wrath
- Sloth
- Avarice
- Gluttony
- Lust

It's not uncommon for Catholics to find themselves in an apologetic encounter with Protestants who want to argue that there are no degrees of sinfulness; that all wrongdoing is equal in God's eyes. Not only is that against the apostle's words—it offends human reason. Of *course* murder is worse than a small lie, stealing is worse than speeding, and so on. Yes, "all wrongdoing is sin," John teaches, but there are some sins that are so serious that they sap the grace of God from our souls, and some that aren't.

This order of the seven Deadlies can help us see the ways in which our souls turn away from God toward disordered infatuation with his creation.

The first three have been called the "cold sins," because this type of sin is locked in on itself, seeing reality only through the wounds of our fallen soul. Do we put ourselves always first? The *proud* person who thinks only of himself is in the coldest and most ungenerous place there is. *Envy* comes in second because at least the envious person recognizes (however perversely) that there is something outside himself that he lacks and longs for. The *wrathful* person is so worked up for what he considers a

Types and Grades of Sin

loss that he shows even more vulnerability by letting his anger manifest his emptiness.

In between these cold sins and the warm sins is the "lukewarm sin" of sloth—not the physical laziness we associate with that word but in fact a spiritual indifference that paralyzes a soul and blinds it to anything great. The *slothful* person instead "wanders" (Aquinas's word) in shallow pursuits—scrolling through social media or spending all night getting to the next level of some video game—leaving the soul even more listless and indifferent to what is truly worthy. The slothful soul never really commits to anything; idolizing potentiality, he is forever leaving options open with the lifelong mantra, "I could have *if*..." This kind of spiritual torpor marks one who has chronically missed out on life.

The "warm sins" begin with *avarice* or greed, habitual for the kind of person who reduces everything to competition and counting. Not just *I want this much money* but *I have this many Facebook followers* or *I finally moved into this zip code*. But as disordered as such counting is, it's understandable that we would want to amass the goods we need to live. Even more understandable in this sense is our need for food and drink; thus *gluttony*—the misuse of material appetites—ranks in deadliness after avarice. After gluttony, the least of the deadly sins both mirrors (the reason it is least) and mocks (the reason it is a mortal sin) the very purpose of our existence: personal union. *Lust* is a fallen desire that renders God's children as two-dimensional objects (the internet does this literally), robbing others of their dignity to be approached with a trusting transparency and not a salacious self-interest.

As a prayer exercise, read the Parable of the Prodigal Son (Luke 15:11–32). Do you see how the younger son represents "the warm sins" of avarice, gluttony, and lust? Yet who is able to return to the Father? The older son personifies pride, envy, and wrath and it is much more difficult for him to let his father embrace him. With which son does your pattern of sinfulness tend to coincide?

ACT OF CONTRITION

✠ O my God, I am heartily sorry for
having offended thee,
and I detest all my sins because of
thy just punishments,
but most of all because they offend thee, my God,
who art all good and deserving of all my love.
I firmly resolve, with the help of thy grace,
to sin no more and to avoid the near occasion of sin.

The Christian response to sin is always necessary, but it need not be dire. For even before we turn back to God, he draws near to us, the sinner. And, if we allow him, God can use even our failings and faults to his glory and for our good. Romans 8:28 says that "all things work for good for those who love God," and St. Thomas says this includes even our sins, for "God makes all things work together for their good to the extent that if they deviate and stray from the path, he even makes this contribute to their good." God's power to create from nothing is the same power able to bring good (a real something) out of sin (a privation, a nothing).

Types and Grades of Sin

For when we rebel against the Lord, his grace can still use those moments to have us rise from our sins in greater humility and cautious awareness of how self-centered we really are. This renewed awareness should result also in a greater wisdom in knowing our constant need for God's grace to persevere in the good. As Aquinas continues: those who sin and repent "return to themselves more humble and wiser; for they fear extolling themselves or trusting in their powers to persevere."

The Four Sins Crying to Heaven for Vengeance

- *Willful Murder* (including abortion): "Then the Lord asked Cain, 'Where is your brother Abel?' He answered, 'I do not know. Am I my brother's keeper?' God then said: 'What have you done? your brother's blood cries out to me from the ground'" (Gen. 4:9–10).

- *The Sin of Sodom*: "So the Lord said: The outcry against Sodom and Gomorrah is so great, and their sin so grave, that I must go down to see whether or not their actions are as bad as the cry against them that comes to me. I mean to find out'" (Gen. 18:20–21).

- *Oppression of the Poor*: "You shall not wrong any widow or orphan. If ever you wrong them and they cry out to me, I will surely listen to their cry." (Exod. 22:21–22).

- *Defrauding Laborers of Their Fair Wage*: "You shall not exploit a poor and needy hired servant, whether one of your own kindred or one of the resident aliens who live in your land, within your gates. On each day you shall pay the servant's wages before the sun goes down, since the servant is poor and is counting on them. Otherwise the servant will cry to the Lord against you, and you will be held guilty" (Deut. 24:14–15).

Despite what skeptics may charge, our Catholic faith never shirks from the problem of evil. What it refuses to do, however, is to place the blame at the top with God or at the bottom with material things themselves. God is good, and so is everything he has made. The problem of evil lies in the *middle*: with we who are free to use our will to choose good or evil, life or death (cf. Deut. 30:19).

Perhaps this world would have continued unfallen if only God had made automata instead of persons—androids who were programmed never to err. But what would it say about God if he had chosen to create robots unable to leave Eden rather than free lovers who can choose holiness? It is a logical conundrum: God could not have created other selves without the possibility of those free selves going freely self-ish. For freely choosing to become gift is the goal of life, the end purpose of our being created in the image of the self-donating divine Persons of the Trinity.

The Six Sins Against the Holy Spirit

- Presumption of God's Mercy
- Despair
- Impugning the Known Truth
- Envy at Another's Spiritual Good

Types and Grades of Sin

- Obstinacy in Sin
- Final Impenitence

The Nine Ways of Being an Accessory to Another's Sin

- By Counsel
- By Command
- By Consent
- By Provocation
- By Praise or Flattery
- By Concealment
- By Partaking
- By Silence
- By Defense of the Wrong Done

Because we are made in the image and likeness of God (Gen. 1:26), we become our truest selves the more we become like God. This is one more way that Christianity is not a religion that was "invented" or imposed unnaturally, but one that really corresponds to the way we have been made.

When we defend the Faith in apologetics, therefore, we are defending the integrity of all creation— not for its own sake, but because it (like the Faith) is God's gift to his children. We are meant to enjoy the sun and the wind, the fur and fleece and fish and flora; all the sights and smells of this created world. The world is the home, the *domus* in Latin, for those made in God's image. This is why Adam was made a lord (*dominus*) and Eve a lady over it.

> God destined the earth and all it contains for all men and all peoples so that all created things would be shared fairly by all mankind under the guidance of justice tempered by charity. This principle is based on the fact that the original source of all that is good is the very act of God, who created both the earth and man, and who gave the earth to man so that he might have dominion over it by his work and enjoy its fruits (cf. Gen. 1:28–29). God gave the earth to the whole human race for the sustenance of all its members, without excluding or favoring anyone.
>
> — COMPENDIUM OF THE SOCIAL DOCTRINE OF THE CHURCH

As the perfect lover, God has given humanity an unmatchable gift in the cosmos as well as an even greater gift—the ability to act *godly* in the ongoing working of the world, including and especially the ability to bring about new life. God has granted men and women a share in his own life and a cooperation in his own proper power. He gave us dominion in order to make this world more beautiful, more full of life.

The Human Drama — From Goodness to Perfection

> Whoever sneers at beauty's name as if she
> were the ornament of a bourgeois past—
> whether he admits it or not—can no longer
> pray, and soon will no longer be able to love.
>
> — HANS URS VON BALTHASAR

In an amazing declaration, the Church teaches that the human person is the only creature on earth whom God willed for his or her own sake, and that to be fully human is thus to imitate God and make oneself a gift of love.

As both human history and our own personal stories attest, this is not an automatic endeavor! There is a drama built into the human person's path to perfection that other creatures do not have. Fallen man teeters between choosing the good (for which he is made) and choosing evil (which diminishes his nature).

> The cow eats grass anywhere and never eats
> anything else. In short, the cow does fulfill the
> materialist theory of history: that is why the cow
> has no history. "A History of Cows" would be one
> of the simplest and briefest of standard works. But
> if some cows thought it wicked to eat long grass
> and persecuted all who did so; if the cow with the
> crumpled horn were worshipped by some cows
> and gored to death by others; if cows began to
> have obvious moral preferences over and above a
> desire for grass, then cows would begin to have a

history. They would also begin to have a highly unpleasant time, which is perhaps the same thing.

— G.K. CHESTERTON

Do you read Scripture closely enough to have noticed that at the last line of Genesis 1, marking the day on which man is created, does not receive its own unique "and it was good"? Out of all the days of creation, only here does God not look at his work for that day but instead reviews "everything he had made." What might this mean? Were Adam and Eve created incompletely?

Perhaps it means that, man and woman being the one creatures on earth with reason and free will, God made them good but wanted to await their own free assent to loving him and one another perfectly—a foreshadowing, St. Augustine mused, of "something yet to come."

Along with all other beings, we are created good; *unlike* all other creatures, however, we are created *not yet complete.* We have been created to *become like God,* and the beginning of that decisive journey commences with our free surrender to him, opening ourselves to the grace to become gift and thereby fulfilling our supernatural end in service of God and neighbor.

> Here we can think of indeed, the Lord Jesus, when he prayed to the Father, "that all may be one . . . as we are one" (John 17:21–22) opened up vistas closed to human reason, for he implied a certain likeness between the union of the divine Persons, and the unity of God's sons in truth and charity. This likeness reveals that man, who is the only creature

The Human Drama — From Goodness to Perfection

on earth which God willed for itself, cannot fully find himself except through a sincere gift of himself.

— GAUDIUM ET SPES

Angels were created for the sake of the whole of creation, and the physical universe was then created for the sake of living things. Those living things manifest their own hierarchy—as soil made for the grass, the grass for the sake of herbivores, those herbivores for the sake of omnivores, and so on. But only man was made for his own sake.

When a couple finds out that they will be new parents, they rush to get the house in order—converting that old room into a new nursery, stocking up on all the provisions a baby needs. Perhaps this is how we can envision the first days of creation: the great Father lovingly and methodically preparing a place for his coming sons and daughters.

Like the children of any loving father, we are freely given everything we need to lead flourishing lives. We are not programmed to embrace lives of virtue, yet nonetheless everything in our lives has been ordered to the fulfillment of that hope of imitating God by becoming a self-gift. What does this mean in practice? In this world filled with married people, celibates and singles, with pipefitters and financiers, the aged and the newborn, it means to discover where God is calling *you* and, with as much prudence and spiritual wisdom you can, to order all relationships and all gifts in your life, vocation and career, toward that end.

> God beholds you. He calls you by your name.
> He sees you and understands you as he made
> you. He knows what is in you, all your peculiar

> feelings and thoughts, your dispositions and likings, your strengths and your weaknesses. He views you in your day of rejoicing and in your day of sorrow. He sympathizes in your hopes and your temptations. He interests himself in all your anxieties and remembrances, all the risings and fallings of your Spirit.
>
> — ST. JOHN HENRY NEWMAN

Notice here a seeming paradox. God made the world for us, to be our home and dominion. All creatures exist for our sake. And yet, since we are created in the image and likeness of God and thus to fulfill our nature we must strive to be his visible reflections, in this world we are fundamentally incomplete. As wonderfully furnished with beautiful beings as this universe is, *no creature can fulfill us.* Our self is so capacious that nothing in the created cosmos, not all the vast universe itself, *nothing,* can satisfy us, ever.

God alone can satisfy our heart, because he created us for the sake of nothing in this world, but for himself.

> You stir us so that praising you may bring us joy, because you have made us and drawn us to yourself, and our heart is unquiet until it rests in you.
>
> — ST. AUGUSTINE

What else does this craving, and this helplessness, proclaim but that there was once in man a true happiness, of which all that now remains is the

empty print and trace? This he tries in vain to fill
with everything around him, seeking in things
that are not there the help he cannot find in those
that are, though none can help, since this infinite
abyss can be filled only with an infinite and
immutable object; in other words by God himself.

— BLAISE PASCAL

The Greek word for "image" is *eikon,* from which we also get *icon.* An icon is a visible representation of a more profound reality. We look at our computer's icons to get to the app or program that the figure represents. Christians gaze upon icons during prayer to recall the Lord, the Mother of God, and the saints in heaven to whom their images point.

Our being made in God's image, then, means we are his icons. We represent God to everyone who sees us, and they to us. If the human person is the icon of God on earth, then, this means every man, woman, and child we meet are God's representatives on earth. We have never met, have never talked to, have never *debated with,* a mere human. We are all the vicars of Love on earth.

BE BORN IN US, INCARNATE LOVE
Caryll Houselander

✠ Be born in us,
Incarnate Love.
Take our flesh and blood,
and give us your humanity;

take our eyes, and give us your vision;
take our minds, and give us your pure thought;
take our feet and set them in your path;
take our hands,
and fold them in your prayer;
take our hearts
and give them your will to love.

At the end of his *Divine Comedy*, Dante described God as the love who moves the entire cosmos. As he reaches the heights of heaven, he wants to know how he, as an image of God, has fit into the divine pattern. Not yet equipped to grasp the complete answer—not having "the wings for such a flight"—Dante's mind is given a glimpse of the truth, "cleaving my mind in a great flash of light," and he feels his "being turned . . . by the Love that moves the sun and the other stars."

> Love is patient, love is kind. It is not jealous, [love] is not pompous, it is not inflated, it is not rude, it does not seek its own interests, it is not quick-tempered, it does not brood over injury, it does not rejoice over wrongdoing but rejoices with the truth. It bears all things, believes all things, hopes all things, endures all things. Love never fails.
>
> — 1 CORINTHIANS 13:4–8A

PRAYER TO LOVE SOMEONE

[This is a very helpful prayer to say regarding anyone in our life, including those to whom we are trying to defend and explain the Faith.]

✠ Lord, give me the grace to love NAME patiently.
Lord, give me the grace to be more kind in my words and actions toward N.
Lord, free me from my jealousy toward/about N.

Lord, I am too proud regarding N.; give me the grace to see this as your gift and not my accomplishment.
Lord, forgive me when I am rude, especially toward N.
Lord, help me at those times when I am feeling stressed, anxious, or impatient when I am with N.
Lord, when I am overly concerned with my self-interest regarding N., allow me to hand over this part of my life to you so I may increase in charity.

Lord, grant me the grace to see you and thus to forgive these old injuries from N.
Lord, forgive me for taking delight in my enemies' failures, and open my heart never to rejoice over N's errors.
Lord, give me the grace to believe and to hope in those you let me love, and temper my uncharitable doubts and suspicions regarding N.

Lord, grant me the graces of hope and loving perseverance in my relationship with you and with N., that we may both someday see your salvation.

Lectio Divina

Lectio (Latin for "reading") is an ancient way of letting God's words speak to you as personally and as uniquely as possible. Normally, this practice takes scenes from the scriptures and allows them to serve as an opportunity to see our own life's journey as an extension of God's activity in history. Try it in these steps:

1. Select a brief passage that draws you; perhaps this could be the Gospel reading for the Mass that day.

2. Contemplate the passage slowly, hovering over any word or phrase or scene that strikes you. The key here is not to get through the passage but to let the Spirit talk to you at whatever point or for however much time you think is enough to savor all that he wants to show you here.

3. Next, ask the Holy Spirit why this particular place in the biblical scene is resonating within you. What word, what image, what teaching is staying with you . . . and why? Is there anything in your memory that amplified this feeling or is there something coming up in your life that made this moment considerably significant at this time?

4. If you are in the habit of (or would like to start) keeping a prayer journal (a sort of spiritual diary), this would be the time to jot down what has happened and what you and the Holy Spirit were just discussing.

In that spirit, let us here consider Luke's account of Jesus and his disciples on the road to Emmaus (chapter 24). The scene begins, as does every authentic Christian moment, in a pilgrim encounter with the risen Lord. Dejected and defeated, two folks slink off away from Jerusalem. On their way, they unknowingly meet the Christ who has, unbeknownst to them, defeated all death. This initial encounter then begins to unfold through the typological fullness of the Old Testament being explained by this still unrecognized prophet: "Was it not necessary that the Messiah should suffer these things and enter into his glory? Then beginning with Moses and all the prophets, he interpreted to them what referred to him in all the scriptures" (Luke 24:26–27).

And then the scriptures gave way to the breaking of bread: "And it happened that, while he was with them at table, he took bread, said the blessing, broke it, and gave it to them. With that their eyes were opened and they recognized him, but he vanished from their sight" (Luke 24:30–31).

This movement, from the Liturgy of the Word to the Liturgy of the Eucharist, results in the third moment of this post-paschal scene. With the disciples' sanctified souls now finally burning with zeal and understanding (Luke 24:32–33), they return to the life they had just recently fled from. Only now, after the word and sacrament have taken root in their hearts, are they equipped to go back into the world to spread and defend the new Christian faith.

This encounter with Jesus helps us understand too why so much of the spiritual life consists in prayerful reflection and remembrance. We cannot know what will occur in the future, and most often we are too "close" to the present for us to understand it fully. Only by looking back on our day, examining our life through a regular retreat, by making a self-examination every evening, can we begin to understand how Christ is talking to us—how he wants to make our hearts burn with the knowledge and power of how God has fulfilled his promises to us and the world.

Allow these three moments to become matter for your prayer and growth in holiness. The Word of God appears and entrusts himself to his followers, even entrusting his very self to the bread he holds—and becomes. This same historical encounter is continued and extended throughout all the world for all time, proclaimed in the scriptures and celebrated in the Eucharist. Thus Jesus extends the same saving work of the road to Emmaus for you to partake of by which to be transformed into his likeness (cf. 2 Pet. 1:4).

> Then let us arise! Scripture invites us in the words, "It is full time now for you to wake from sleep" (Rom. 13:11). With our eyes open to the light that transfigures, our ears filled with the thunder of his voice, let us listen to the powerful voice of God, urging us day by day, "Oh, that today you would hearken to his voice! Harden not your hearts" (Ps. 95:8). And again: "He who has an ear, let him hear what the Spirit says to the churches" (Rev. 2:7). And what does he say? "Come, O children, listen to me, I will teach you the fear of

Lectio Divina

the Lord" (Ps. 34:11). "Walk while you have the light, lest the darkness overtake you" (John 12:35).

Moreover, the Lord, in seeking among the crowd for someone to work for him, says, "Who is there who desires life?" (Ps. 34:12). If you hear him and answer, "I do," God says to you, 'Do you desire true life, eternal life?" then: "Keep your tongue from evil, and your lips from speaking deceit. Depart from evil, and do good; seek peace, and pursue it" (Ps. 34:13–14). And when you have done this, I will set my eyes upon you, I will give ear to your prayers, and "Before they call, I will answer" (Isa. 65:24).

— ST. BENEDICT OF NURSIA

3

God Comes to His People

> I did not tell you this from the beginning,
> because I was with you.
>
> But now I am going to the one who sent me, and
> not one of you asks me, "Where are you going?"
>
> But because I told you this, grief has filled
> your hearts.
>
> But I tell you the truth, it is better for you that I
> go. For if I do not go, the Advocate will not come
> to you. But if I go, I will send him to you.
>
> — JOHN 16:4B–7

The two main characteristics of charity are to do good for one's beloved and to live in union with him or her. Using images drawn from friendship as well as marriage, Jesus tries to tell us how closely united with us he longs to be. It was to the end of this unity that he became eternally united to us by taking a human nature. The goal of this section is to pray and reflect through the meaning of the Incarnation and the presence of the Holy Spirit—in our lives and in our work defending the truth about the Lord's humanity and earthly mission.

Do we worship a God of power or a God of love? Do we understand love's need to come to us in humility and not in might?

God loves us more than we love ourselves. We are not a distraction or a burden to God; he *longs* to be with us. We are loved, redeemed, one in whom God himself rejoices.

> The Lord, your God, is in your midst, a
> mighty Savior, who will rejoice over you
> with gladness, and renew you in his love,
> who will sing joyfully because of you.
>
> — ZEPHANIAH 3:17

To prove this, he has become just like us. For us—for *you*—a divine person has chosen to live a life of a hungry, tired, mortal working man. To seal this union, the Father also sends his Holy Spirit to live in us: to be the loving principle of our life just as he is in the life of the Holy Trinity.

We take seriously—and we proclaim and defend as good—the created order as God's first gift to his people. Beyond that and even more importantly, God has elevated and ennobled the created order by uniting it to his divine nature in the

And the Word Became Flesh

Incarnation. Every embodied being, all of time and space, and everything that fills this cosmos were never the same after.

This means, practically, that all things now have the potential of bringing us closer to Jesus Christ. That is why, for most people and probably for you, holiness will be realized nowhere other than where you are right now—probably not in the monastery, most likely not in extreme acts of asceticism, but in the very life God has set out for you in this moment.

God, the great lover, desires not only good for us but intimate union with us. Why? Perhaps because *intimacy* leads to *identity*. We tend to become like the people we are around the most. And that is why, as wonderful as the technology that makes seeing and talking and texting to our close companions is, there is no substitute for being with them in person, in the flesh.

Caro cardo salutis.
(The flesh is the hinge of salvation.)
— TERTULLIAN

The word for flesh in Latin is *caro, carnis,* from which we get *incarnation,* and in Christ's incarnation the in-the-flesh principle of personal union takes on a radically perfect, fourth-dimensional meaning. Because of it, our bodies, our minds and emotions and desires, all the concrete stuff of creation, may become more closely identified with him. They may be *sanctified*.

THE SOUL OF APOLOGETICS

THE ANGELUS
[Traditionally recited daily at 6 a.m., Noon, and 6 p.m.]

✠ V/. The angel of the Lord declared unto Mary
R/. And she conceived of the Holy Spirit.

Hail Mary, full of grace, the Lord is with thee;
blessed art thou among women,
and blessed is the fruit of thy womb, Jesus.
Holy Mary, Mother of God, pray for us sinners
now and at the hour of our death.

V/. Behold the handmaid of the Lord
R/. Be it done unto me according to thy word.
Hail Mary . . .

V/. And the Word was made flesh
R/. And dwelt among us.
Hail Mary . . .

V/. Pray for us, O holy Mother of God,
R/. That we may be made worthy of
 the promises of Christ.

Let us pray. Pour forth, we beseech thee, O Lord,
thy grace into our hearts; that we, to whom the
Incarnation of Christ thy Son was made known by the
message of an angel, may by his passion and cross
be brought to the glory of his resurrection.
Through the same Christ our Lord.

And the Word Became Flesh

The created order is thus the groundwork for God's greatest work in the coming of his Son as the God-man. That divine descent into matter bookended and confirmed God's creation of the world as a good place with meaning and purpose. In the Word, all things were made, and without him nothing came to be (John 1:3). In the Word made flesh, all things are re-made; what is good by nature can be made perfect by grace.

> Behold, I make all things new.
>
> — REVELATION 21:5

In Christ, all things now speak to us of God's providential care and unconditional love. When God himself was a man on earth, he looked around and saw how even the birds of the air were provided for (Matt. 6:26; 10:29), how the lilies of the field were more beautiful than any regal garments (Matt. 6:28–29), and how even the hairs on our heads testify to God's providence.

And the end of that providence is not to give us our daily bread or even to save us from our sins. God became man not simply to provide for and heal us but to make us *holy*, participants in his own divine life (1 Pet. 2:4–5).

> See! The Lord is our mirror:
> open your eyes,
> look into it,
> learn what your faces are like!
>
> — ODES OF SOLOMON

> Only in Christ do we find real love, and the fullness of life. And so I invite you today to look to Christ. When you wonder about the mystery of yourself, look to Christ who gives you the meaning of life.
>
> — ST. JOHN PAUL II

Created in God's image in the Beginning, our faces have been re-imaged into Christ's by nothing other than his love. For when we survey human history or the day's headlines, we see how mean and desiccated and envious our species is. Even close to our hearts we find innumerable jealousies, petty fears, and secret plans for revenge. So much of ourselves is scared and self-centered, unwilling to let love get too close.

The Christian account of how this came to be is found back in Genesis when the first couple turned away from God's invitation to intimacy with him. In so rebelling, Adam and Eve fated all their progeny to a doomed course. It is as if one of your ancestors had gambled away a magnificent sum of cash which could have been your inheritance if he had not acted so foolishly so many years ago. But instead of abandoning us to ourselves, God decided to recreate the human race by starting over with a new Adam and a new Eve.

> Therefore, just as through one person sin entered the world, and through sin, death, and thus death came to all, inasmuch as all sinned—for up to the time of the law, sin was in the world, though sin is not accounted when there is no law. But death reigned from Adam to Moses, even over those who did not sin after the pattern of the trespass of

A New Adam ... and a New Eve

> Adam, who is the type of the one who was to come. Grace and Life through Christ. But the gift is not like the transgression. For if by that one person's transgression the many died, how much more did the grace of God and the gracious gift of the one person Jesus Christ overflow for the many.
>
> — ROMANS 5:12–15

So, each of us belongs to two Adams: the first representing our disobedience and disdain for the good, and remind us of our lost spiritual inheritance, and the second directing us toward charity and mercy and all that Christ embodies. In him, we have been *recapitulated*—given a new head (Eph. 1:10)—and can now share in the Son's perfect love of the Father and his for us.

As there is a first and second Adam, so too with Eve. Our blessed mother Mary, the second Eve, remedies the first Eve's selfishness by her love and humble obedience.

> He became man by the virgin, in order that the disobedience which proceeded from the serpent might receive its destruction in the same manner in which it derived its origin. For Eve, who was a virgin and undefiled, having conceived the word of the serpent, brought forth disobedience and death. But the Virgin Mary received faith and joy, when the angel Gabriel announced the good tidings to her that the Spirit of the Lord would come upon her, and . . . the Holy Thing begotten of her is the Son of God.
>
> — ST. JUSTIN MARTYR

> When I remember the disobedience of Eve, I weep. But when I view the fruit of Mary, I am again renewed. Deathless by descent, invisible through beauty, before the ages light of light; of God the Father was thou begotten; being Word and Son of God, thou didst take on flesh from Mary virgin, in order that thou might renew afresh Adam fashioned by thy holy hand.
>
> — ST. GREGORY THE WONDERWORKER

> Death came through Eve, but life has come through Mary.
>
> — ST. JEROME

The name *Eva* (in Latin) is renewed into *Ave*, the greeting of Gabriel to Mary (Luke 1:28). Where the first Eve was deceived by a fallen angel, the second was enlightened by one of God's most trusted messengers. And where the first brought about death through disobedience beneath the tree in Eden, the second led to life being given upon the tree of Calvary. That is why the early Church Fathers saw in Genesis 3:15, in the aftermath of the Fall, the *Protoevangelium* or "first gospel." There the Lord forewarns Satan, "I will put enmity between you and the woman, and between your offspring and hers; They will strike at your head, while you strike at their heel."

The second person of the Trinity takes our human nature to himself through the "yes" of Mary, the second Eve. Her *fiat*—"let it be done"—is the watershed moment in all human history

A New Adam . . . and a New Eve

(Luke 1:38). Having been preserved from the dissolution and division that are the result of original sin—for the Father had preserved her from conception for this single moment—she is able to offer the Son of God humanity in its fullness.

> Once something has been bound, it cannot be loosed except by undoing the knot in reverse order . . . And so the knot of Eve's disobedience was untied by Mary's obedience. What Eve bound through her unbelief, Mary loosed by her faith.
>
> — ST. IRENAEUS

Good prayer comes from good theology. We can never separate spirituality from study, devotion from dogma, just as we can never divide defending the Faith from loving our neighbor. From Irenaeus's millennia old Mariology comes a most beautiful novena: to Mary, Undoer of Knots. This devotion arose in Germany around 1700, prompted by a painting depicting Mary untying the knots of a chord and returning the rope back to earth smooth and renewed to her children.

TO MARY, UNDOER OF KNOTS

✠ Dearest holy mother, most holy Mary,
you undo the knots that suffocate your children.
Extend your merciful hands to me.

I entrust to you today this knot
[mention your request here]

and all the negative consequences that it
provokes in my life.
I give you this knot that torments me
and makes me unhappy
and so impedes me from uniting myself to you and
your Son Jesus, my Savior.
I run to you, Mary, Undoer of Knots,
because I trust you
and I know that you never despise a sinning child
who comes to ask you for help.

I believe that you can undo this knot because Jesus
grants you everything.
I believe that you want to undo this knot
because you are my mother.
I believe that you will do this because you love
me with eternal love.
Thank you, dear mother.

Just as God began the new era in Christ with a woman, it is a pious practice for each of his children to begin their day with this same woman, our mother Mary. Since she is the one who gave the Son of God his body and all its senses, it is also fitting to consecrate all of ourselves to her.

The God-Bearer

ACT OF CONSECRATION TO MARY

✠ My queen and my mother, I offer myself
entirely to you this day.
Pray that I have the grace to consecrate to you
the use of my eyes, ears, mouth, heart, words and
thoughts, and my entire being.
You hold me as your child, form me also into a more
faithful friend of your son Jesus.
This alone will make me a fit and fruitful friend
in your loving hands and in his service,
bringing the greatest possible salvation for me
and for other souls,
and glory to God our Father.

Whereas the first two ecumenical councils (Nicaea in 325 and I Constantinople in 381) were dedicated to understanding the Persons of the Trinity, the next two were compelled to take up the question of Jesus' being both God and man, and how he is related to humanity. This arose because in the early 400s the people of God were being forbidden, in isolated parts of the Church, to invoke Mary as the "mother of God."

"How can God have a mother?" some small-minded bishops and influential monks mocked the faithful. Certainly, God the Son does not have a mother—for he is Son eternally, begotten from the Father before all time. Yet it's just as certain that the Son incarnate, Jesus Christ, true God and true man, was conceived in the womb of and borne by his mother Mary. And because Jesus is God—a single divine person who fully possesses both divine and human nature—it is logical and right to say that Mary is whom the Greeks name *Theotokos*, the God-bearer. Or, in Latin, *Mater Dei*, the mother of God.

SUB TUUM PRAESIDIUM ("Under Your Protection," c. A.D. 300)

✠ We turn to you for protection,

Holy mother of God.

Listen to our prayers

and help us in our needs.

Save us from every danger,

glorious and blessed Virgin.

In 431, Emperor Theodosius II called for a council to address the heresy being pushed by the influential archbishop of Constantinople, Nestorius. Though quite comfortable calling upon Mary as the *Christokos*—the bearer of Christ—Nestorius forbade anyone to invoke Mary as *Theotokos*. This heresy of dividing the divine person into two severable natures, now known as Nestorianism, is still evident today in many forms, especially in modern theology that likes to separate the "Jesus of history" from the "Christ of faith."

At such times of peril, God always sends a faithful viceroy—as he sent Athanasius at Nicaea and the Cappadocian Fathers to I Constantinople. And now St. Cyril of Alexandria appeared at the Council of Ephesus. With the full support of Pope Celestine I, Cyril charged Nestorius with heresy and explained to the gathered council fathers that calling Mary "mother of God" is non-negotiable because it expresses the truth that Jesus Christ is one person who truly took human nature to his divine self.

INVOCATION OF THE BLESSED MOTHER

✠ Mary, most holy virgin and
mother, look down upon me!
I have now received your most dear Son.
You conceived him in your immaculate womb,
you gave birth to him,
and you nursed him and enfolded him with
most loving embraces.
Humbly and with love I now present to you
anew this Son of yours.
his very appearance brought you joy and filled
you with all delight.
I offer him to you, that you may hold him
again in your arms and
love him with all your heart.

I do this as an act of worship of the most Holy Trinity,
and I offer him for your honor and
glory, that through him
my needs and those of the whole
world may be fulfilled.

> I ask you, most dear Mother, to obtain for me
> forgiveness of all my sins,
> the grace of serving Jesus most
> faithfully from now on,
> and the gift of final perseverance, so that with you I
> may praise him forever.

By virtue of that divine person whom she bore, this mystery is also reason to give Mary the highest honor possible for a created being. Where Christians offer God the adoration or worship due to him alone (Greek: *latria*), and rightly give honor (*dulia*) to all the saints, to Mary we express *hyperdulia*—a kind of super esteem—recognizing her singular role as a saved creature (Luke 1:47) in salvation itself.

VENERATION OF MARY
Attributed to St. Cyril of Alexandria

✠ Hail, Mother and virgin, eternal
temple of the Godhead,
venerable treasure of creation, crown of virginity,
support of the true faith,
on which the Church is founded
throughout the world.

Mother of God, who contained the infinite
God under your heart,

whom no space can contain:

through you the most holy Trinity is revealed,
adored, and glorified,

demons are vanquished, Satan cast down
from heaven into hell

and our fallen nature again assumed into heaven.

Through you the human race, held captive in
the bonds of idolatry,

arrives at the knowledge of truth.

What more shall I say of you?

Hail, through whom kings rule, through whom the
only begotten Son of God

has become the star of light to those sitting in
darkness and in the shadow of death.

In the course of these heated months of debate, Cyril sent theologically packed letters to Nestorius explaining the Church's position. In the third and richest of these missives, Cyril laid out twelve essential Christological doctrines that every believer must hold. Each ends with a warning that failure to profess it would make you anathematized—excommunicated, cut off from ecclesial communion until the heresy held is recanted.

The use of *anathema* biblically based (e.g., Acts 23:14; 1 Cor. 12:3, 16:22; Rom. 9:6; Gal. 1:8–9) and historically has been used neither to punish nor to cut someone off forever but to urge reformation of mind and mores. Cyril's intent was to help Nestorius see that the connection between Jesus' divine and human natures is not based simply on association or agreement but on real unity with the second Person of the Trinity. That is why Cyril uses the very Greek term *hypostasis*—from a Greek word for "person"—to indicate the intimate inseparability of Jesus' two natures.

> The Word is united hypostatically to flesh, so we worship one Son and Lord Jesus Christ, neither putting apart and dividing man and God, as joined with each other by a union of dignity and authority. That is, taking flesh of the holy virgin, and making it his own from the womb, he underwent a birth like ours, and came forth a man of woman, not throwing off what he was, but even though he became a man by the assumption of flesh and blood, yet still remaining what he was, that is, God indeed in nature and truth.
>
> — ST. CYRIL OF ALEXANDRIA

Cyril helped the Church explain the Incarnation as a personal (*hypostatic*) union between the Son of God's eternal, uncreated divine nature and his temporal, created human nature. The second Person of the Trinity now acts in these two natures: never in tension, always in tandem. Jesus wasn't a blended "God-human hybrid." *But,* we can say with full truth that God—a divine Person—truly became man and so truly has a mother.

> If anyone does not confess that Emmanuel is God in truth, and therefore the holy Virgin is Theotokos—for she bore in the flesh the Word of God become flesh—let him be anathema.
>
> If anyone does not confess that the Word of God the Father was united by hypostasis to flesh and is one Christ with his own flesh, that is, the same both God and man together, let him be anathema.
>
> — ST. CYRIL OF ALEXANDRIA

At Mary's "yes," God did not change—but we did! The God-man took all that is human to himself, and thus injected his own divine sonship into every human life. It is now possible to become a child of the Father and child of Mary in a mystical but real sense. As Vatican II put it, Mary "is our mother in the order of grace" (*Lumen Gentium* 61). We can therefore reach out to her for comfort with perfect hope and confidence.

> It is enough, O Virgin, to be called the Mother of God. It suffices to be the nurse of him who nurtures the world and a great thing to have held within your womb the One who upholds all things.
>
> — AMPHILOCIUS OF ICONIUM

THE SOUL OF APOLOGETICS

MEMORARE

✠ Remember, O most gracious Virgin Mary,
that never was it known that anyone who
fled to thy protection,
implored thy help, or sought thy
intercession, was left unaided.
Inspired by this confidence, I fly unto thee,
O virgin of virgins, my mother.
To thee do I come, before thee I stand,
sinful and sorrowful.
O Mother of the Word Incarnate,
despise not my petitions,
but in thy mercy hear and answer me.

> The Blessed Virgin Mary was nearest to Christ in his humanity, because he received his human nature from her. Therefore, it was due to the Virgin Mary to receive a greater fullness of grace than others.
>
> — ST. THOMAS AQUINAS

PRAYER OF ST. JOHN PAUL II TO MARY

✠ May you who are the servant of the Lord,
be our example of a humble and generous

welcome of the will of God!
You who are the mother of sorrows at
the foot of the cross,
be there to lighten our loads
and wipe away the tears of those afflicted by
family difficulties.

May Christ the Lord, king of the
universe, king of families,
be present, as at Cana, in every Christian home,
to communicate his light, joy, serenity, and strength.
May every family generously add its share to the
coming of his kingdom on earth.
To Christ and to you, Mary, we entrust our families.

Not long before the Council of Ephesus, St. Augustine drew from his years as a professional orator to make the analogy of how the Incarnation can be compared to *speaking our minds*. When we speak a word, it is not that mental word that changes but all that is added to it in order to make that otherwise silent word known in space and time: the air, the shape of our mouths and use of our tongue and teeth, and so on.

> That which we have in mind is expressed in
> words and is called speech. But our thought is
> not transformed into sounds; it remains entire
> in itself and assumes the form of words by

means of which it may reach the ears without suffering any deterioration in itself. In the same way the Word of God was made flesh without change that he might dwell among us.

— ST. AUGUSTINE

Christ's incarnation and that celebrated birth at Bethlehem did not change God; it changed the world. For it was only the first part of what was to happen. The second part is that now that the divine has become united with humanity, humanity may become united with divinity.

FOR AWARENESS OF GOD'S PRESENCE IN EVERY MOMENT

✠ Heavenly Father, you sent your Son into
 the world you created.
 You love us so much that you give us not only this world with all that is in it,
 but now even your own divine life is made available in all that we are and in all that we can do.

 Show me what it would mean for me to
 live a holier life:
 how to be more conscious of your presence, more grateful for your gifts,
 and more loving throughout my day.

Without Confusion or Change, Division or Separation

Twenty years after Ephesus, the Church was compelled to gather yet again to tackle a new heresy: the idea that Jesus' divinity was so powerful that it overwhelms his humanity—and so he really has only one (*mono*) nature (*physis*). This was the heresy of *monophysitism*.

At the Council of Chalcedon in 451, an influential monastery superior named Eutyches held that all the human experiences and emotions of Jesus nonetheless belonged to a nature unlike other humans because it was consumed by his divinity. Jesus, then, was consubstantial with God the Father but not with his human brothers and sisters.

The Church Fathers at Chalcedon knew that this was contrary to Scripture and to the entire purpose of the Incarnation. But how should they explain how divinity and humanity can dwell perfectly and wholly in one person? If Jesus wasn't a hybrid, what does it mean to say that God can die or that a man can now perform miracles?

The shorthand Christology that arose from the deliberations at Chalcedon aimed to teach four key truths about Jesus' divinity and humanity:

1. They do not interfere with each other.

2. They never morph into the other.

3. They never act in isolation from one another.

4. They belong to one person, not two disconnected entities.

These absolute principles became known as the *four Chalcedonian adverbs* necessary when speaking of the union of Jesus' divinity and humanity: that these two natures act *without confusion, without change, without division,* and *without separation.*

These guardrails ensure that we always understand Christ as one divine person who assumed a whole human nature to himself (complete with body and soul) without ever foregoing his divine personhood and divine nature. Jesus was conceived in Mary's womb but did not become a "person" there—for he is eternally the second person of the most Holy Trinity. And that divine person has chosen to live forever after as a man while remaining fully God.

THE KENOTIC HYMN

Have among yourselves the same attitude that is also yours in Christ Jesus,
Who, though he was in the form of God,
did not regard equality with God
something to be grasped.
Rather, he emptied himself, taking
the form of a slave,
coming in human likeness; and found
human in appearance,
he humbled himself, becoming obedient to death,
even death on a cross.
Because of this, God greatly exalted him and
bestowed on him the name

Without Confusion or Change, Division or Separation

> that is above every name, that at the name of Jesus
> every knee should bend,
> of those in heaven and on earth and under the earth,
> and every tongue confess that Jesus Christ is Lord,
> to the glory of God the Father.
>
> — PHILIPPIANS 2:5–11

One of the great heroes of Chalcedon, Pope Leo, was not even in attendance: Pope Leo, but in a letter popularly known as *The Tome* (officially, *Letter 28 to Flavian*), Leo beautifully laid out the mechanics of this divine condescension.

> Accordingly while the distinctness of both natures and substances was preserved, and both meet in one Person, lowliness is assumed by majesty, weakness by power, mortality by eternity; and in order to pay the debt of our condition, the inviolable nature was united to the passible, so that, as the appropriate remedy for our ills, one and the same "Mediator between God and men, the man Christ Jesus," might from one element be capable of dying, and from the other be incapable. Therefore, in the entire and perfect nature of very man was born very God, whole in what was his, whole in what was ours.
>
> – POPE LEO I

The Church came to call this crucial doctrine the *communication of idioms*. It means that whatever we "communicate"—say—about Christ in one of his natures, we can also communicate about him in the other. We can say that "God thirsted" and "God died," and also that "a man has power over creation" and "a man can raise the dead." Of course, the divine nature cannot die, and the human nature cannot defeat death. In Jesus Christ, however, one Person with a divine nature was subject to suffering and the same person with a human nature is lord of the universe.

> Christian, remember your dignity, and now that you share in God's own nature, do not return by sin to your former base condition. Bear in mind who is your head and of whose body you are a member. Do not forget that you have been rescued from the power of darkness and brought into the light of God's kingdom.
>
> Through the sacrament of baptism, you have become a temple of the Holy Spirit. Do not drive away so great a guest by evil conduct and become again a slave to the devil, for your liberty was bought by the blood of Christ.
>
> — POPE LEO I

This profound theology runs through the first four Church councils, reflecting the deepest heart of Christianity. Out of love for his wayward children, the Father sends his Son to be

The Incarnation Fills Every Moment with Grace

no longer just consubstantial with him but now consubstantial with a human mother and all the human race. Jesus loves you so much, he became just like you.

> For we do not have a high priest who is unable to sympathize with our weaknesses, but one who has similarly been tested in every way, yet without sin.
>
> — HEBREWS 4:15

Dwell on that for a moment: everything you do that is not sinful—your waking up, taking care of your bodily needs, your circle of friends, career, spouse and kids, your hobbies and pastimes—are all things to which God has joined himself. This means that we can meet God *wherever we are*, in *whatever we do*. He is not out there in some distant, hidden plan for our life that we have to search for; he is not to be found only in religious or ceremonious practices. He is there throughout your day and in the very life he is asking you to lead *right now*.

Christianity is not simply about reaching heaven in the future; it's about consecrating every aspect of your humanity and the world in which you inhabit right now. Just as Jesus consecrated humanity and inhabited the world, and as he fills both with his grace today.

MORNING PRAYER OF ST. BASIL THE GREAT

✠ As I rise from sleep I thank thee, O Holy Trinity,
  for through thy great goodness and patience thou was not angered with me,

an idler and sinner, nor hast thou
destroyed me in my sins,
but hast shown thy usual love for men.
And when I was prostrate in despair,
thou hast raised me to keep the morning watch
and glorify thy power.

Now enlighten my mind's eye and open my mouth
to study thy words and understand thy
commandments and do thy will,
and sing to thee in heartfelt adoration and praise
thy most holy name of Father, Son and Holy Spirit,
now and ever, and to the ages of ages.

We said that the ultimate purpose of apologetics is not to win an argument or even to reach agreement on some fine theological point; it is to bring others closer to Jesus Christ and his Church. The same God-man Jesus who lived with us on earth in a definite time and place is the same God-man in heaven: still longing to be one with each of us, still thirsting for our response of love.

This is where holiness begins, in the passivity of our surrender. God will not bring about our response if we do not allow him; and without that response of surrender, intimacy with God (or indeed with other humans) is impossible. Pray for the grace to make that response to him!

Now We are God's Friends and Brothers

PRAYER OF ADORATION

St. Alphonsus Liguori

✠ My crucified love, my dear Jesus!
I believe in thee, and confess thee to be the true Son of God and my Savior.
I adore thee from the abyss of my own nothingness, and I thank thee for the death you suffered for me, that I might obtain the life of divine grace.

My beloved Redeemer, to thee I owe all my salvation.
If I have not loved thee in times past, I love thee now; and I desire nothing but to love
thee with all my heart.
But without thy grace I can do nothing.
Since thou hast commanded me to love you,
give me also the strength to fulfil this, your sweet and loving precept.

Vatican II teaches that Jesus Christ not only reveals God to us but shows us who *we ought to be*. The new Adam is the perfect man, not only our guide but our goal. He embodies what we are called to become.

> The truth is that only in the mystery of the incarnate Word does the mystery of man take on

> light . . . Christ the Lord. Christ, the final Adam, by the revelation of the mystery of the Father and his love, fully reveals man to man himself and makes his supreme calling clear. For by his incarnation the Son of God has united himself in some fashion with every man. He worked with human hands, he thought with a human mind, acted by human choice and loved with a human heart. Born of the Virgin Mary, he has truly been made one of us, like us in all things except sin.
>
> — *GAUDIUM ET SPES*

In calling us "friends," Jesus revolutionized the way we think of God. For the ancients, the gods could not be friends with men because a friend is "another self," as Aristotle put it. To the pre-Christian mind, there is too much distance, too much separation between the perfection of the gods and the neediness of mankind, rendering friendship impossible. Yet in becoming human, Jesus calibrated God's perfection to our poverty: "For you know the gracious act of our Lord Jesus Christ, that for your sake he became poor although he was rich, so that by his poverty you might become rich" (2 Cor. 8:9).

PRAYER OF THANKSGIVING

Jean Cardinal Daniélou

✠ O Jesus, who for love of me
consented to become man,
I thank you with all my heart.

Now We are God's Friends and Brothers

O Jesus, who for love of me, passed nine months in the bosom of a Virgin,
I thank you with all my heart.
O Jesus, who for love of me willed to be born in a poor stable,
I thank you with all my heart.
O Jesus, who for love of me worked in the sweat of your brow,
I thank you with all my heart.
O Jesus, who for love of me suffered a painful passion,
I thank you with all my heart.
O Jesus, who for love of me hung on the Cross for three hours and died in ignominy on it,
I thank you with all my heart.
O Jesus, who from the Cross gave me Mary to be my mother,
I thank you with all my heart.
O Jesus who ascended to heaven, to prepare a place for me and to make yourself my advocate with the Father,
I thank you with all my heart.
O Jesus, who for love of me reside day and night in the tabernacle,
I thank you with all my heart.

> O Jesus, who for love of me immolate yourself every morning on the altar,
> I thank you with all my heart.
> O Jesus, who come so often into my heart by holy communion,
> I thank you with all my heart.
> O Jesus, who in the holy tribunal so often wash me in your precious blood,
> I thank you with all my heart.

If you tend to romanticize the Lord's appearance on earth, remember how he spent thirty years in obscurity, laboring through the aches and pains of life just like all of us. Remember that he spent his mere three years in ministry being ridiculed by the "wise" and persecuted by the "pious." Remember how he spent his last few days being rejected by friends and subjected to horrifying torture and anguish. Remember how he finally let go of everything to endure an ignoble death on the cross for the sake of those who deserved none of his love and mercy.

> Jesus, I have come to know that you do not want me to distinguish my sins from the other sins of the world, but to enter more deeply into your heart and consider myself responsible for the sins of those persons whom you may wish . . . anyone else as it may please you. You make me feel, Jesus, that I must descend even lower, take with me the sins of others, accept as a result all the punishments, that these may draw down upon me from your justice,

Now We are God's Friends and Brothers

and in a particular way the disdain of the persons for whom I will offer myself. To accept, or rather to long for dishonor, even in the eyes of those whom I love. To accept the great abasements, of which I am not worthy, in order to be ready at least to accept the small ones. Then, Jesus, my charity will resemble that with which you have loved me.

— JEAN CARDINAL DANIÉLOU

In the initial throes of romance, grandiose gestures rule the day: the young man plays every part the gentleman—opening doors, bringing flowers, bedazzling with polite manner. As love grows, the majestic yields to the mundane—lover and beloved free to share what is truly important to them, in trust and transparency revealing even weaknesses and wounds.

The people of God have had this same experience. When we were first getting to know the one true Lord, we encountered a God who sought our undivided allegiance through incredible feats and monumental miracles: the dividing of seas (Exod. 14:21–31; Jos. 3:14–17), the demolishing of other deities (1 Kings 18:20–40), or the sun moving at his behest (2 Kings 20:9–11; Isa. 38:7–8). Yet, by the time of the beginning of Jesus' public ministry, God openly joins the line of sinners who have gathered to be baptized by John (Matt. 3:13–17); toward the end of his ministry, God becomes a slave who washes feet (John 13:1–17) and willingly becomes a convicted criminal to be executed.

These moments help to reveal the great paradox of Christianity: in the full plan of his love, the Almighty chose to save each of is not through his omnipotence but through his powerlessness.

THANKS BE TO THEE
Attributed to St. Richard of Chichester

☩ Thanks be to thee, my Lord Jesus Christ
For all the benefits thou hast given me,
For all the pains and insults thou hast borne for me.
O most merciful Redeemer, friend and brother,
May I know thee more clearly,
Love thee more dearly,
Follow thee more nearly.

Was it not Satan who tempted Jesus to use his divine power to overcome weak human things like bodily hunger, a lust for power, and the fear of being injured (Matt. 4:1–11)? How easily Jesus could have proven his divine strength! How forcefully he could have squashed the enemy! Yet he chose to be bound to his human limitations and inevitable mortality. This is the love of the Incarnation: the love of smallness, the love of the cross. This is how the kingdom of God and not man is built. As the preface for the Feast of Christ the King puts it, "A kingdom of truth and life, a kingdom of sanctity and of grace, a kingdom of justice, of love, and of peace."

> Cross, sanctified by the body of Christ, good cross, long desired always, I loved you and wished to embrace you. Welcome me and bring me to my Master.
>
> — LAST WORDS ASCRIBED TO ST. ANDREW

The Cradle Leads to the Cross

None of us can escape what it means to be human. *Aequat omnes cinis,* said Seneca: "The ashes make us all equals." Jesus did not escape it, either—and did not seek to escape it, though he could have. He knows that we always inch toward death, and he wants to meet us not only in the joys and consolations of life but whenever doubt and despair can take hold of our fragile soul.

The world separates the cross from joy. Suffering is an irredeemable evil. But the Christian knows that our joy is realized wherever Jesus is; wherever Jesus places you.

> The love of the cross in no way contradicts being a joyful child of God. Helping Christ carry his cross fills one with a strong and pure joy, and those who may and can do so, the builders of God's kingdom, are the most authentic children of God . . . Only in union with the divine head does human suffering take on expiatory power. To suffer and to be happy although suffering, to have one's feet on the earth, to walk on the dirty and rough paths of this earth and yet to be enthroned with Christ at the Father's right hand, to laugh and cry with the children of this world and ceaselessly to sing the praises of God with the choirs of angels: this is the life of the Christian until the morning of eternity breaks forth.
>
> — ST. TERESA BENEDICTA OF THE CROSS

Unlike Jesus, we tend to find God repugnant and sin alluring. So, Jesus has come to model for us not a way to dominate our world but to live humbly in it, not standing tall in a Promethean pose over evil but kneeling meekly before God. Where the gods of old were known by their power, by thunderbolts and hammers in their hands, Jesus shows us a God who is powerful enough to be known by the nails in his.

> There is a certain usefulness to temptation. No one but God knows what our soul has received from him, not even we ourselves. But temptation reveals it in order to teach us to know ourselves, and in this way we discover our evil inclinations and are obliged to give thanks for the goods that temptation has revealed to us.
>
> — ORIGEN

God allows us to be tempted because it is a way of leading us to realize how really insufficient we are by ourselves. Temptations show us how much we need God's grace to be Christians—to be *fully ourselves*. He allows temptations to humble us (but never humiliate us) by revealing bit by bit how proud and self-sufficient we really try to be. Temptations help us understand our own weaknesses and how the enemy of our human nature attacks us—and thus become opportunities to form better strategies for avoiding sin.

> Without supernatural aid I would hardly be a human being.
>
> — ATTRIBUTED TO EVELYN WAUGH

The Cradle Leads to the Cross

PRAYER AGAINST TEMPTATION
St. Alphonsus Liguori

✠ Behold me, O my God, at thy feet!
I do not deserve mercy, but O my Redeemer, the
blood which thou hast shed for me
encourages me and obliges me to hope for it.
How often have I offended thee, repented, and yet
have I again fallen into the same sin!

O my God, I wish to amend; and in order to
be faithful to thee,
I will place all my confidence in thee.
I will, whenever I am tempted, instantly
have recourse to thee.

Before, I have trusted in my own
promises and resolutions,
and have neglected to recommend myself to
thee in my temptations.
This has been the cause of my repeated failures.
From this day forward, be thou, O Lord, my strength;
and thus shall I be able to do all things,
for "I can do all things through him
who strengthens me."

The cross of Jesus Christ is the ultimate proof of God's love for us—for we who are so often gladly tempted and who freely fall. "Only with difficulty does one die for a *just* person," writes St. Paul. Yet "God proves his love for us in that *while we were still sinners* Christ died for us" (Rom. 5:6–8). From his ultimate vulnerability in the womb of Our Lady to his last breath on the cross, Jesus is the first to give his heart entirely to another: eternally to the Father and forever to each of us as our head and Savior. This is the triumph of tenderness.

The Fourteen Stations of the Cross

1. Jesus is Condemned to Death

2. Jesus is Made to Bear His Cross

3. Jesus Falls the First Time

4. Jesus Meets His Mother

5. Simon Helps Jesus Carry His Cross

6. Veronica Wipes Jesus' Face

7. Jesus Falls the Second Time

8. Jesus Meets the Women of Jerusalem

9. Jesus Falls the Third Time

The Cradle Leads to the Cross

10. Jesus is Stripped

11. Jesus is Nailed to the Cross

12. Jesus Dies on the Cross

13. Jesus is Taken Down from the Cross

14. Jesus is Laid in the Tomb

This is why Catholics employ a crucifix and not just an empty cross as the main sign of the one true faith. Everyone *wants* an empty cross. Everyone can love what is clean and beautiful and seemingly perfect. Only the Lord and the saints can love what is weak, hurting, bloody and broken. Only Christ can infuse the human heart with the grace needed to do it.

TRADITIONAL PRAYER BEFORE A CRUCIFIX

✠ Look down upon me, good and gentle Jesus
while before your face I humbly kneel and,
with burning soul, pray and beseech you
to fix deep in my heart lively sentiments
of faith, hope, and charity;
true contrition for my sins,
and a firm purpose of amendment.
While I contemplate, with great love and tender pity,
your five most precious wounds,

THE SOUL OF APOLOGETICS

pondering over them within me
and calling to mind the words which David,
your prophet, said to you, my Jesus:
"They have pierced my hands and my feet,
they have numbered all my bones."

> The cross is the war memorial against the demons, the sword against sin, the blade that Christ used to prick the serpent. The cross is the will of the Father, the glory of the only begotten Son, the Spirit's transport of joy, the world of angels, the safety of your Church, the boast of Paul, the wall of the saints, the light of the whole earth. Today we have beheld our Lord Jesus Christ on the altar. Today we have grasped the coal of fire of which the Cherubim sang in a shadow. Today we have heard that great and sweetest voice crying out. This is the body that burned off the thorns of sins and enlightens human souls. This is the body the woman with a hemorrhage touched and was delivered from her suffering. This is the body which the daughter of the Canaanite woman saw and was healed. This is the body that the prostitute, by approaching with her whole soul, wiped away the filth of her sins. This is the body that Thomas when touching cried out "My Lord and My God." This is the body that brought us so great and wondrous a salvation.
>
> — ST. JOHN CHRYSOSTOM

We Are the New Temples of the Presence

It is a sad mystery why we don't more easily surrender to love. Freely willed self-alienation is an all-too-common but undetected sin. For some reason, we tend to wallow in our self-destruction—content to say that *the world I have built for myself isn't the greatest world, but at least it's mine!*

Perhaps that is what we fear in surrendering to another: no longer being the center of our own lives. Or perhaps we fear facing the realization that everything we thought was so important was not so essential after all.

> Let us lie in wait for the righteous one, because he is annoying to us; he opposes our actions, reproaches us for transgressions of the law and charges us with violations of our training. He professes to have knowledge of God and styles himself a child of the Lord. To us he is the censure of our thoughts; merely to see him is a hardship for us, because his life is not like that of others, and different are his ways. He judges us debased; he holds aloof from our paths as from things impure. He calls blest the destiny of the righteous and boasts that God is his Father.
>
> — WISDOM 2:12–16

After all our disappointments, though, what remains is the care and the love Jesus has for you. He will never, never cast aside those willing to come to him. Pray to understand deeply how God calls you as you are and where you are in life right now.

Do not wait; do not think you have disappointed him. Let your heart be pierced, acknowledging not only your need for grace but the delight you give God when you allow him to love you.

If personal closeness is a mark of charity, it is not surprising that God arranged to have his Holy Spirit live personally and intimately in those who have surrendered to Christ. Although the Spirit of God was active in the formation of God's first chosen people, Jesus reveals a new presence of his Holy Spirit— no longer given mainly to some for a particular time and task but now imparted to all the faithful, without distinction, for the sake of our regeneration and sanctification. It is this universality that makes God's people Catholic.

The Spirit is thus the "glue" who binds together the mystical body of saints and saints-to-be. He does this by taking up residence in the souls he sanctifies by his indwelling. Perhaps one of the harder truths Paul's Jewish audience had to contend with was his preaching that the great temple in Jerusalem did not contain the divine but now the *souls of the baptized* were the new places of God's presence. Now that the Almighty had taken on human flesh and become one of his own, in our neighbor where we met the God who has become man. And the Holy Spirit's indwelling is the sign and seal of that holy presence.

> Do you not know that your bodies are members of Christ? Shall I then take Christ's members and make them the members of a prostitute? Of course not! [Or] do you not know that anyone who joins himself to a prostitute becomes one body with her? For "the two," it says, "will become one flesh." But whoever is joined to the Lord becomes one spirit

The Holy Spirit Animates Apologetics

with him. Avoid immorality. Every other sin a person commits is outside the body, but the immoral person sins against his own body. Do you not know that your body is a temple of the Holy Spirit within you, whom you have from God, and that you are not your own? For you have been purchased at a price. Therefore, glorify God in your body.

— 1 CORINTHIANS 6:15–20

COME, HOLY SPIRIT

✠ Come, Holy Spirit, fill the hearts of your faithful
and kindle in them the fire of your love.
Send forth your Spirit and they shall be created,
and you shall renew the face of the earth.

O God, who have taught the hearts of the faithful
by the light of the Holy Spirit,
grant that in the same Spirit we may be truly wise
and ever rejoice in his consolation.

Through Christ our Lord.

As we thirst for greater prayer and intimacy with the Lord, we turn to the Holy Spirit: "In the same way, the Spirit too comes to the aid of our weakness; for we do not know how to pray as we ought, but the Spirit itself intercedes with inexpressible groanings" (Rom. 8:26–27). Because his role in salvation is "to come to our aid," the Holy Spirit is fittingly revealed to us as our Consoler and even our Advocate—the person of the Trinity who most aptly assures us of God's loving care and whose role it is to speak on our behalf, our divine advocate before the Father.

PRAYER OF CONSECRATION
Fr. Felix Rougier

✠ Most Holy Spirit, receive the consecration that I
make of my entire being.
From this moment on, come into every area of my life
and into each of my actions.
You are my light, my guide, my strength, and the sole
desire of my heart.

I abandon myself without reserve to
your divine action,
and I desire to be ever docile to your inspirations.
O Holy Spirit, transform me, with and through Mary,
into the image of Christ Jesus,
for the glory of the Father and the
salvation of the world.

Apologetics—persuasively speaking the truth about God—is ultimately an act of love, helping other human beings see the liberating splendor of a life in Christ. Praying to the Holy Spirit to exert a welcoming influence in the minds of those we engage

The Holy Spirit Animates Apologetics

is an essential part of this work. It is no coincidence that four of the seven gifts of the Holy Spirit pertain to the refining of our human intellect—understanding, knowledge, wisdom, and counsel all aim to unite what we naturally know with the supernatural cause of all that is.

PRAYER FOR THE SEVEN GIFTS OF THE HOLY SPIRIT

✠ Lord Jesus Christ, who, before
ascending into heaven,
did promise to send the Holy Spirit
to finish your work
in the souls of your apostles and disciples,
deign to grant the same Holy Spirit to me that he
may perfect in my soul
the work of your grace and your love.

Grant me the spirit of wisdom that I may despise the
perishable things of this world
and aspire only after the things that are eternal,
the spirit of understanding to enlighten my mind
with the light of your divine truth,
the spirit of counsel that I may ever choose the
surest way of pleasing God and gaining heaven,
the spirit of fortitude that I may
bear my cross with you
and that I may overcome with courage all the

obstacles that oppose my salvation,
the spirit of knowledge that I may know
God and know myself
and grow perfect in the science of the saints,
the spirit of piety that I may find the service of
God sweet and amiable,
and the spirit of fear that I may be filled with a loving
reverence toward God
and may dread in any way to displease him.

Mark me, dear Lord, with the sign of
your true disciples
and animate me in all things with your Spirit.

In your apostolate of apologetics, ask the Holy Spirit to increase his gifts in you, the very graces you received at baptism. The graces of baptism infused you not only with the theological virtues of faith, hope, and charity, but also the seven gifts of the Holy Spirit as well as his twelve fruits: *gifts* because they are God's special ways of making us more docile to hear, love, and follow him in all things, and *fruits* because they are foretastes of the heavenly life itself.

> *GIFTS OF THE HOLY SPIRIT*
> (ISAIAH 11:1–3)
>
> Piety, Understanding, Fortitude, Wisdom,
> Counsel, Knowledge, and Fear of the Lord

The Holy Spirit Animates Apologetics

FRUITS OF THE HOLY SPIRIT (GALATIANS 5:22–23)

Charity, Joy, Peace, Patience, Counsel, Knowledge, and Fear of the Lord, Humility, Fidelity, Modesty, Continence, and Chastity

The lists may not line up exactly with modern translations of the Bible, as the earliest Old Testament readings of Isaiah were based on the Greek Septuagint, and Galatians 5 on St. Jerome's Latin Vulgate which contain ancient yet variant readings. Regardless, these effects of the Holy Spirit have been given to you to assist your vocation as a Christian and are available to those whom you have been called to befriend and evangelize. Ask the Holy Spirit to purify your intellect and to sharpen your speech while opening the minds of those to whom you have been called to share the truths of Christ.

PRAYER FOR PROPAGATION OF THE FAITH

✠ O Holy Spirit, you desire the
salvation of all human beings
and for that purpose you want all of them to acquire
the knowledge of your truth.
Grant to all of them your powerful light and
your love of goodwill
that they may give glory to God in unity of
faith, hope, and love.
Send laborers into the harvest who are

truly animated by you,
who are the soul of the missionary Church.

ACT OF FAITH

✠ O my God, I firmly believe that you are one God in three divine Persons,
Father, Son and Holy Spirit.
I believe that your divine Son became human and died for our sins,
and that he will come again to judge the living and the dead.
I believe these and all the truths that the holy Catholic Church teaches,
because you, who cannot deceive nor be deceived, revealed them.

ACT OF HOPE

✠ O my God, relying on your almighty power and infinite mercy and promises,
I hope to obtain pardon of my sins, the help of your grace, and life everlasting,
through the merits of Jesus Christ,
my Lord and Redeemer.

The Ancient Jesus Prayer

ACT OF CHARITY

✠ O my God, I love you above all things, with my whole heart and soul,
because you are all good and worthy of all my love.
I love my neighbor as myself for the love of you.
I forgive all who have injured me and ask pardon of all whom I have injured.

An ancient and often forgotten prayer is simply to repeat the inspired petition, "Lord Jesus Christ, Son of God, have mercy on me, a sinner."

This prayer dates back to at least the fifth century, as various forms of it have been found etched in caves throughout the Egyptian desert, and John Chrysostom (d. 407) recommended a variant of it: "Lord Jesus Christ, Son of God, have mercy." What has come to be known as the "Jesus Prayer" begins with the recognition of our need for mercy and aims to match the power of reciting Jesus' holy name with the rhythm of our breathing.

The Jesus Prayer thus takes very seriously St. Paul's injunction to "pray without ceasing" (1 Thess. 5:17). It also recalibrates what we think of as "prayer"—from something we "do" perfunctorily and at prescribed places and times to something we "become." To be a person of prayer means that our entire day is filled with the lifting of our minds to the awareness of God's active presence and the surging of our hearts in gratitude to him.

The Jesus Prayer is based on the power of the very name of Jesus. "Because of this, God greatly exalted him and bestowed on him the name that is above every name, that at the name of Jesus every knee should bend, of those in heaven and on earth and under the earth, and every tongue confess that Jesus Christ is Lord, to the glory of God the Father" (Phil. 2:9–11). Angels rejoice in this name, and demons fear it. His name alone has the healing power to calm and soothe the anxious soul. Its mere repetition reminds us to whom we belong and who is the Master of our souls.

Have you ever *really* prayed in the holy name of Jesus? He promises us that those who do will know a whole new power of God. This name answers our doubts and opens our souls to receive all that God longs to give us "On that day you will not question me about anything. Amen, amen, I say to you, whatever you ask the Father in my name he will give you. Until now you have not asked anything in my name; ask and you will receive, so that your joy may be complete" (John 16:23–24).

> The spirit, when we close all its outlets by our concentration on God, demands of us expressly some task that may satisfy its need for activity. It should therefore be given the *Jesus Prayer* as the only occupation that answers fully to its purpose. It is, in fact, written that "No one can say 'Jesus is Lord' except by the Holy Spirit" (1 Cor. 12:3) . . . Those who meditate on this holy and glorious name continually in the depths of their heart can see also the light of their own spirit. For if it is entertained with great care by the mind, the name with intense emotion destroys all the impurities that cover the

The Ancient Jesus Prayer

> surface of the soul. In fact, it is said, "The Lord your God is a devouring fire" (Deut. 4:24). Consequently, the Lord now transports the soul to a great love . . . . This name . . . is the pearl of great price; on discovering it, one rejoices with unspeakable joy, and sells all one's possessions in order to purchase it.
>
> — DIADOCHUS OF PHOTIKE

The Jesus Prayer is a way of allowing the Holy Spirit, the one who enables you to confess Jesus as Lord, to breathe in and out of you. Such deep meditation begins to conform to your very being, breathing in as you pray, "Lord, Jesus Christ, Son of God," and exhaling while praying, "Have mercy on me, a sinner." Eventually the power of Jesus' name takes root in our very being and it can become a connatural part of our busy days.

The Jesus Prayer may also be considered a form of white or hidden martyrdom. It is a hidden way of denying yourself the way of the world by not always indulging your senses in shallow pursuits. Instead of using that brief moment at a stoplight to check text messages or scroll through social media, for example, let the Jesus Prayer rise again to your consciousness and become a moment of divine intimacy before the green light calls you back to your normal activities. Unbeknownst to the world, recitation of the Jesus Prayer becomes a sweet asceticism, a casual but powerfully hidden intimacy between you and the Trinity alone.

Finally, the Jesus Prayer is a way of taking seriously the gospel's admonitions to "stay vigilant" (Matt. 24:42). It is how we keep the presence of God ever in our hearts—which because of original sin are ever in conflict between the ways of the world and the ways of our Savior. As a prayer of the heart, the Jesus Prayer allows us to unite the otherwise mundane moments of our day with the presence and providence of God.

> The heart is but a small vessel; and yet dragons and lions are there, and there poisonous creatures and all the treasures of wickedness; rough, uneven paths are there, and gaping chasms. There likewise is God, there are the angels, the heavenly cities and the treasures of grace; all things are there.
>
> — ST. MACARIUS

When a woman is pregnant with her child, her entire world changes. She is now aware that she is no longer just herself but has been entrusted with an immortal other. She is now this little one's nourishment, shelter, teacher, guide, and defender. Everything about her day—meals, sleep, exercise, and all that she takes in through her senses—is now measured by what is good for another.

Or, when an athlete trains seriously for an event, every moment of his day changes. Meals now become opportunities to feed his muscles, so he is conscious of what he eats; sleep is the needed respite which repairs any injuries, so he disciplines himself to get the right amount; his entire daily routine centers around the end goal of successfully completing the challenge before him.

Likewise, when one is immersed in the Jesus Prayer, everything in life is altered. Now meals become sacramentals, sleep and awaking become symbols of death and resurrection, personal interactions echo the Visitation, and other mundane events harken other divine mysteries. In such a life the beggar mirrors the hungry Christ, the shut-in is the lonely Christ thirsting for attention, the innocence of a child echoes the infant Jesus lying in the hearts of all.

The Jesus Prayer thus infuses into our everyday lives the divine company of Jesus and the saints. His holy name becomes the lens through which we begin to see the order of reality as the Father does, replete with the life of his Son who has come to redeem every aspect of this world.

Following the practice of the Christian East, try dedicating ten minutes a day to the Jesus Prayer. Find a prayer position that is comfortable but not irreverent, and, having for those ten minutes put all else out of mind, simply recite, "Lord Jesus Christ, Son of God, have mercy on me, a sinner" slowly, intentionally, and consciously.

Before long, you will no doubt notice a reduction in anxiety and in your usual tendency to be distracted. Over time and with diligence, these words can become part of your breathing, yielding a natural conformity between you and your soul, body, and the powerful and holy name of Jesus. From these moments of grounding your day in Christ, the Jesus Prayer will naturally begin to appear throughout the day as well, especially at those times where you seek some internal rest and spiritual nourishment.

STAY WITH ME
St. John Henry Newman

✠ Stay with me, and then I shall begin to shine as thou shinest: so to shine as to be a light to others. The light, O Jesus, will be all from thee. None of it will be mine. No merit to me. It will be thou who shinest through me upon others. O let me thus praise thee, in the way which thou dost love best, by shining on all those around me. Give light to them as well as to me; light them with me, through me. Teach me to show forth thy praise, thy truth, thy will. Make me preach thee without preaching—not by words, but by my example and by the catching force, the sympathetic influence, of what I do—by my visible resemblance to thy saints, and the evident fulness of the love which my heart bears to thee.

4

Christ's Body, the Church

When Jesus went into the region of Caesarea Philippi he asked his disciples, "Who do people say that the Son of man is?" They replied, "Some say John the Baptist, others Elijah, still others Jeremiah or one of the prophets." He said to them, "But who do you say that I am?" Simon Peter said in reply, "You are the Messiah, the Son of the living God." Jesus said to him in reply,

"Blessed are you, Simon son of Jonah. For flesh and blood has not revealed this to you, but my heavenly Father. And so I say to you, you are Peter, and upon this rock I will build my Church, and the gates of the netherworld shall not prevail against it. I will give you the keys to the kingdom of heaven. Whatever you bind on earth shall be bound in heaven; and whatever you loose on earth shall be loosed in heaven."

> Then he strictly ordered his disciples to tell no one that he was the Messiah.
>
> — MATTHEW 16:13–20

To understand what Christ intended in founding, sustaining, and directing the Catholic Church, we must grasp that its primary goal is to bestow upon and increase his life in each one of us. The Church is our sharing in his living, mystical body.

> Christ is the whole point of the Church's functioning. We are not baptized into the hierarchy, do not receive the cardinals sacramentally, will not spend eternity in the beatific vision of the pope . . . Christ is the point.
>
> — FRANK SHEED

Believing that Christ founded the Church, Catholics are both blessed and burdened by having to explain to the world how the operations of this Church truly reflect the will of Jesus for his people; how continuity with the first apostolic band is found in the Church's bishops; how the rites instituted by Jesus persist in the Catholic sacraments; how the Lord's teachings are faithfully formulated and preserved in Catholic doctrine.

> I am writing you about these matters, although I hope to visit you soon. But if I should be delayed,

The Marks of the Church

> you should know how to behave in the household of God, which is the church of the living God, the pillar and foundation of truth.
>
> — 1 TIMOTHY 3:14–15

At the First Council of Constantinople in 381, the Church Fathers affirmed something the Nicene Creed did not see a need to make explicit: the divine origin and sustenance of the Church. In those intervening decades, the teaching authority of the Church had come under fire by disgruntled heretics and, consequently, the Fathers and Constantinople insisted that any baptized Christian understand that he is being initiated into the *"one, holy, catholic, and apostolic Church."* As we pray before and through our efforts to defend the truth about the Catholic Church, let us reflect on each of these *marks* and the riches they offer.

GOD OUR REFUGE AND OUR STRENGTH

✠ O God! Our refuge and our strength,
 look down with favor on thy people who cry to thee;
 and through the intercession of the glorious and
 immaculate Virgin Mary, mother of God,
 of St. Joseph her spouse,
 of thy blessed apostles Peter and Paul,
 and of all the saints,
 in mercy and goodness hear our prayers for the
 conversion of sinners,

and for the liberty and exaltation of our holy mother the Church. Through the same Christ our Lord.

Oneness

The opposite of Christian unity is not multiplicity but division. There is no more diverse community on earth than the Catholic Church—many cultures, many colors, many careers, but only one creed. Yet the Lord founded one Church: "Blessed are you, Simon son of Jonah. For flesh and blood has not revealed this to you, but my heavenly Father. And so I say to you, you are Peter, and upon this rock I will build my Church, and the gates of the netherworld shall not prevail against it" (Matt. 16:17–18). To be *one,* then, means not to be monolithic but to be integrated, to be whole.

Much of the work of Catholic apologetics is attesting to need for Catholic wholeness. Today there may be many Christian communities but there can be only one Church, *subsisting*—as Vatican II teaches—in the one, holy, Catholic, and apostolic Church.

> With the expression *subsistit in*, the Second Vatican Council sought to harmonize two doctrinal statements: on the one hand, that the Church of Christ, despite the divisions which exist among Christians, continues to exist fully only in the Catholic Church, and on the other hand, that "outside of her structure, many elements can be

found of sanctification and truth," that is, in those churches and ecclesial communities which are not yet in full communion with the Catholic Church.

— *DOMINUS IESUS*

This is why we do not speak of these separated Christian groups (and still less Catholicism) as "denominations"—mere names by which we differentiate basically equal representatives of Christ's Church. And this is why we must prayerfully contemplate St. Cyprian's well-known expression, "Outside the Church, there is no salvation" (*extra ecclesiam, nulla salus*). For this ancient doctrine can be either a club used to batter a foe or a loving witness to the integrity of Christ's body on earth. Just as the saving elements of the Catholic Church overflow into other Christian communities, our love of God must overflow into love of all our brothers and sisters.

BE KIND TO YOUR CHILDREN
Attributed to St. Clement of Alexandria

✠ Be kind to your little children, Lord;
that is what we ask of you as their Tutor,
you the Father, Israel's guide; Son, yes,
but Father as well.
Grant that by doing what you told us to do,
we may achieve a faithful likeness to the image and,
as far as is possible for us,
may find in you a good God and a lenient judge.

> May we all live in the peace that comes from you.
> May we journey toward your city, sailing through the waters of sin untouched by the waves,
> borne tranquilly along by the Holy Spirit, your wisdom beyond all telling.
> Night and day until the last day of all, may our praises give you thanks, our thanksgiving praise you:
> you who alone are both Father and Son, Son and Father,
> the Son who is our Tutor and our teacher, together with the Holy Spirit.

The Church's wholeness ensures a sanity to its instruction on what to believe and how to live, and a trust that the parts of the mystical body can act in a unified and thus effective and fruitful manner. The cause of such unity is Christ himself, the eucharistic Lord; a sign and symbol of this unity is the priestly hierarchy, those visible faces of Christ's headship.

> See that you all follow the bishop, even as Jesus Christ does the Father, and the presbytery as you would the apostles; and reverence the deacons, as being the institution of God. Let no man do anything connected with the Church without the bishop. Let that be deemed a proper Eucharist, which is administered either by the bishop, or by one to whom he has entrusted it. Wherever the bishop shall appear, there let the multitude

The Marks of the Church

> [of the people] also be; even as, wherever Jesus Christ is, there is the Catholic Church. It is not lawful without the bishop either to baptize or to celebrate a love-feast; but whatsoever he shall approve of, that is also pleasing to God, so that everything that is done may be secure and valid.
>
> — ST. IGNATIUS OF ANTIOCH

Where Christ is, there is his Church. This is the first truth about the Church we must ponder—Christ and his people are one, as the head and the body, as a groom and bride, are one. The Church is not just a human organization striving to be Christlike, it *is* Christ. The Church is not an option or even a superfluity, but God's own intended way of mediating himself to his people. The Church is his Plan A for salvation.

This helps explain the old adage that Protestants find Christ and then decide on a church, whereas Catholics first know the Church and then come to know Christ. As debatable as this line might be (especially when it's leveraged to imply that the Church is an obstacle to knowing Christ), a Catholic should not be bothered by it. The Church *is* where Christ wants to meet us. It is where he placed the scriptures and the sacraments. It is where holy families—domestic churches, the first schools of faith—are forged. It is where his eucharistic presence feeds and animates our souls.

> He who beholds the Church really beholds Christ.
>
> — ST. GREGORY OF NYSSA

Jesus prays that as he and the Father are one, so may his followers be one (John 17:11). Christian unity, then, must imitate the bonds of the Trinity, which means that it must be practically synonymous with *charity*. This approach to unity goes beyond mutual agreement on core matters of faith or morals, and certainly beyond sameness on every theological or liturgical detail. It requires and empowers us to *see in one another the person of Christ*. Accordingly we must hear his own instruction in the teaching of his apostles: "Whoever listens to you listens to me. Whoever rejects you rejects me. And whoever rejects me rejects the one who sent me" (Luke 10:16).

> Separate a ray of the sun from its body of light, its unity does not allow a division of light; break a branch from a tree — when broken, it will not be able to bud; cut off the stream from its fountain, and that which is cut off dries up. Thus also the Church, shone over with the light of the Lord, sheds forth her rays over the whole world, yet it is one light which is everywhere diffused, nor is the unity of the body separated. Her fruitful abundance spreads her branches over the whole world. She broadly expands her rivers, liberally flowing, yet her head is one, her source one; and she is one mother, plentiful in the results of fruitfulness: from her womb we are born, by her milk we are nourished, by her spirit we are animated.
>
> — ST. CYPRIAN OF CARTHAGE

Christ did not come to live and die and rise from the dead for an anonymous collective or for humanity in general, but for *you*. That is why the oneness, the catholicity of the Church begins in each believer's heart. We must not have divided hearts (James 1:7–8), wanting Jesus and not wanting Jesus—or, more commonly, wanting Jesus on our own terms and not on his. To seek a God made in our own image is the first and fundamental rift in the unity of the Church.

Fortunately, the Church exists to guard the integrity of our hearts. The Lord founded it to provide the community, the sacraments and rites, the space and the way of life—to show us unequivocally who we have been created to be. In it, we together—the perfect God and sinful man—coalesce in a school of holiness. This is what St. Augustine called "the whole Christ," when God and man come together—one in condescension, the other in elevation and eventual deification.

> Christ and his Church thus together make up the "whole Christ" (*Christus totus*). The Church is one with Christ. The saints are acutely aware of this unity:
> Let us rejoice then and give thanks that we have become not only Christians, but Christ himself. Do you understand and grasp, brethren, God's grace toward us? Marvel and rejoice: we have become Christ. For if he is the head, we are the members; he and we together are the whole man. . . . The fullness of Christ then is

> the head and the members. But what does "head and members" mean? Christ and the Church.
>
> — ST. AUGUSTINE
>
> Head and members form as it were one and the same mystical person.
>
> — ST. THOMAS AQUINAS
>
> A reply of St. Joan of Arc to her judges sums up the faith of the holy doctors and the good sense of the believer: "About Jesus Christ and the Church, I simply know they're just one thing, and we shouldn't complicate the matter."
>
> — CATECHISM OF THE CATHOLIC CHURCH

The Son of God has become one of us so that we might become the sons and daughters of God. Christ is the Son by his nature, the only-begotten; we become sons and daughters through the grace of adoption. He *is* the "image of the invisible God" (Col. 1:15; Heb. 1:3); we are fashioned after that image (Gen. 1:27). This divine descent is to rouse us to ascend and to begin living like other Christs, continuations of his own love of the Father and love of all humanity.

> Because God has become man, man can become God. He rises by divine steps corresponding to those by which God humbled himself out

The Marks of the Church

of love for men, taking on himself without any change in himself the worst of our condition.

— MAXIMUS THE CONFESSOR

This truth captures the essence of Christianity. God's incarnation is only half the story. The other half is our deification—the final fruit and full flowering of the mystery of God's bridging of divine and human in the person of the God-man Jesus.

> For this is why the Word became man, and the Son of God became the Son of man: so that man, by entering into communion with the Word and thus receiving divine sonship, might become a son of God.
>
> — ST. IRENAEUS

> The only begotten Son of God, wanting to make us sharers in his divinity, assumed our nature, so that he, made man, might make men gods.
>
> — ST. THOMAS AQUINAS

Through sanctifying grace, God's indwelling presence increases Christ's own life within us. To allow this to happen, our first act of becoming Christ, the first action in our being "saved," is to *surrender*. It is that moment when we finally admit that we are lacking, needy, sinful creatures who cannot redeem ourselves. For many of us, this was done by those who first loved us—parents and godparents—at baptism, but it remains the key move daily, to let our hearts melt before the flame of Jesus' Sacred Heart.

SWEET JESUS

✠ Sweet Jesus,
For my sake you became like me so I could
more become like you.

Open my heart to live this grace truly and in all
of my daily actions,
for you long to continue your life in and through me.

Here is the heart of love: to realize that the one to whom we are attracted is the one who we want to be like. How soothing and comforting it is to hear that God himself has loved each of so much that he has become like each of us. All our prayer should be directed toward this kind of transformation.

> When you are at prayer you are in my presence, and I am in yours. Do not be surprised because I say presence; for if you love me—and it is because I am the image of God that you love me—I am as much in your presence as you are in your own. All that you are substantially, that am I. Indeed, every rational being is the image of God. So he who seeks in himself the image of God seeks there his neighbor as well as himself; and he who finds it in himself in seeking it there, knows it

The Marks of the Church

> as it is in every man . . . If then you see yourself, you see me, for I am not different from you; and if you love the image of God, you love me as the image of God; and I, in my turn, loving God, love you. So seeking the same thing, tending toward the same thing, we are ever in one another's presence, in God, in whom we love each other.
>
> — CLAUDIANUS MAMERTUS

The central sacrament of the Church's unity is, perhaps unsurprisingly, one of the central subjects of the Catholic apologist's devoted defense: the Blessed Sacrament. Even at the time when the Christian scriptures were being written, Christians saw in the bread and wine of the Mass the same unity God intended for his people.

> Even as this broken bread was scattered over the hills, and was gathered together and became one, so let your Church be gathered together from the ends of the earth into your kingdom; for yours is the glory and the power through Jesus Christ forever. But let no one eat or drink of your thanksgiving [Eucharist], but they who have been baptized into the name of the Lord; for concerning this also the Lord has said, Give not that which is holy to the dogs.
>
> — THE *DIDACHE*

Let us now ponder how the Church's unity is her holiness, as both are signs of our communion with the triune God here on earth. As the Father and Son are one in the Spirit, we too are called to be one with both God and neighbor, a unity which is achieved only truly in Christian holiness.

Holiness

Because the Church is one with Christ, it partakes of his own holiness.

> For you are praised in the company
> of your saints and, in crowning their
> merits, you crown your own gifts.
> — ROMAN MISSAL, PREFACE I OF THE SAINTS

> Must I exclude my holiness from Christ's? The answer: no; I can be certain that when he speaks, he speaks inseparably from his body. Shall even then I dare to say, I am holy? If I meant "holy" in the sense of making others holy and standing in no need of anyone to sanctify me, I should be arrogant to claim it, and a liar; but if it means "holy" in the sense of "made holy" . . . then, yes, let Christ's body dare to say it.
> Therefore he crowns you because he crowns his own gifts, not your merits.
> — ST. AUGUSTINE

Defending the mark of the Church's holiness, then, is to affirm that Christ is always generous with his grace, longing always to infuse his own divine life in the souls of his disciples. To call the Church *holy* is like complimenting someone for having her mother's eyes. Of course, those eyes are the daughter's; but their existence and their brilliance are total gift, the image of the giver.

PRAYER TO HUMBLY BEG GOD'S GRACE

✠ O my God, you know my great poverty and misery,
and that of myself I can do nothing.
You know how unworthy I am of this infinite favor,
and you alone can make me worthy.

Since you are so good as to invite me to yourself,
add this one bounty more to all the rest—to
prepare me for yourself.
Never let me be guilty of your body and blood by an
unworthy communion.
For the sake of this same precious blood, which
you have shed for me,
deliver me, O Jesus, from so great an evil.

In the early centuries of the Church, great bishops such as Cyprian and Augustine had to defend the holiness of the Church's sacraments from the sinfulness of those sacraments' ministers. For example, since they were most often the first objects of pagan persecution, an unfortunate number of clerics in the early Church capitulated to pagan Rome. This gave rise to the question: does a priest or bishop's treachery invalidate the sacraments he performs for the people?

To sort out the question, the Church adopted the expression *ex opere operato* to signify how the sacraments communicate divine grace. This gave assurance that sacraments were real and valid "out of (*ex*) the work (*opere*) worked (*operato*)," and so did not depend on the moral status of the celebrant of that sacrament. Because the Church is *holy*, through its identification with Christ the source of holiness, baptism and reconciliation and the Eucharist and all the other efficacious signs of grace transcend their human ministers. The priest and the people participate in those divine channels, but Jesus Christ—the reason why the Church is holy—is their true agent, ensuring their validity.

And yet the personal sanctity, disposition, and choices of the human minister or recipient of the sacrament *do* influence the ultimate fruits that our cooperation with those graces produces. And so, the sacraments can also be regarded *ex opere operantis*: out of the work of the (human) worker.

> His divine power has bestowed on us everything that makes for life and devotion, through the knowledge of him who called us by his own glory and power.
>
> — 2 PETER 1:3

Apart from God, we have absolutely nothing. When we surrender to Jesus Christ and freely allow him to work within us, he grants us—through the mediation of the Church, his holy body—all the power we need to live a life pleasing to him. All along it is his perfect grace, his perfect gift; but we encounter that power according to our imperfect individual humanity. Yet, through diligent cooperation with that power, our humanity is perfected, made *saintly*, as we swap out vice for virtue, selfishness for selflessness, a fixation with created things for eyes turned lovingly to God.

PRAYER AFTER HOLY COMMUNION
St. Padre Pio

✠ Stay with me, Lord, because I am weak and I need your strength, that I may not fall so often.
Stay with me, Lord, for you are my life, and without you, I am without meaning and hope.
Stay with me, Lord, for you are my light, and without you, I am in darkness.
Stay with me, Lord, to show me your will.
Stay with me, Lord, so that I can hear your
voice and follow you.
Stay with me, Lord, for I desire to love you ever more, and to be always in your company.
Stay with me, Lord, if you wish me to be
always faithful to you.
Stay with me, Lord, for as poor as my soul is, I wish it to be a place of consolation for you, a dwelling of your love.

Stay with me, Jesus, for it is getting late; the days are coming to a close and life is passing.

Death, judgment and eternity are drawing near.

It is necessary to renew my strength, so that I will not stop along the way; for that I need you.

It is getting late and death approaches.

I fear the darkness, the temptations, the dryness, the cross, the sorrows.

O how I need you, my Jesus, in this night of exile!

Stay with me, Jesus, because in the darkness of life, with all its dangers, I need you.

Help me to recognize you as your disciples did at the breaking of the bread,

so that the eucharistic communion be the light that disperses darkness,

the power that sustains me, the

unique joy of my heart.

Stay with me, Lord, because at the hour of my death I want to be one with you,

and if not by communion, at least by

your grace and love.

Stay with me, Jesus; I do not ask for divine consolations because I do not deserve them,

but I only ask for the gift of your presence.

The Eucharist — Source of an Apologist's Strength

Oh yes! I ask this of you.
Stay with me, Lord, for I seek you alone,
your love, your grace, your will, your heart, your spirit,
because I love you and I ask for no other reward but
to love you more and more,
with a strong active love.
Grant that I may love you with all my
heart while on earth,
so that I can continue to love you perfectly
throughout all eternity, dear Jesus.

At the heart of the Church's holiness is the Lord's enduring bodily presence on its altars and in its sanctuaries: the holy Eucharist.

> "I am the living bread that came down from heaven; whoever eats this bread will live forever; and the bread that I will give is my flesh for the life of the world." The Jews quarreled among themselves, saying, "How can this man give us [his] flesh to eat?" Jesus said to them, "Amen, amen, I say to you, unless you eat the flesh of the Son of man and drink his blood, you do not have life within you. Whoever eats my flesh and drinks my blood has eternal life, and I will raise him on the last day. For my flesh is true food, and my

blood is true drink. Whoever eats my flesh and drinks my blood remains in me and I in him.

— JOHN 6:51–56

The heart of apologetics is love, and God's love is most profoundly revealed in the way the incarnate Lord keeps his promise to be with us always, "until the end of the age" (Matt. 28:20). The Son of God has assumed our flesh and blood, and he assured us that he would never leave us orphans (John 14:18). That same flesh and blood thus remain with us, and they still physically commune with us, until the world passes and is renewed. The Eucharist is the Church's ground and goal, its source and summit. In the celebration of Mass, the salvific deeds of Calvary are re-presented. There, the Lamb of God continues to pour out his blood as the one true sacrifice that saves the world.

> The Eucharist is "the source and summit of the Christian life." The other sacraments, and indeed all ecclesiastical ministries and works of the apostolate, are bound up with the Eucharist and are oriented toward it. For in the blessed Eucharist is contained the whole spiritual good of the Church, namely Christ himself, our Pasch.
>
> — CATECHISM OF THE CATHOLIC CHURCH

The Eucharist — Source of an Apologist's Strength

O SACRUM CONVIVIUM

✠ *O sacrum convivium,*
 O sacred banquet,

 in quo Christus sumitur,
 wherein Christ is received

 recolitur memoria passionis eius,
 the memory of his passion renewed,

 mens impletur gratia,
 the mind is filled with grace,

 et futurae gloriae nobis pignus datur.
 and the pledge of future glory is given unto us.

There has never been, and there can never be, a successful apologist or evangelist who did not root his efforts in the holy Eucharist.

How do you prepare yourself for Mass? Do you actively participate in the liturgy with your intentional concentration on its prayers and postures? Do you prepare your soul to commune with Christ's with regular confession, and do you receive him with physical and spiritual reverence? Do you make a regular visit to eucharistic adoration?

> No one would touch a royal garment with unclean hands, even if he were in a desert, or alone, even if no one were present, although there was no other

garment or the web of a worm. If you are amazed at dye, this is only the blood of a dead fish. But at the same time, no one would choose to approach him boldly with filthy hands. But if someone would not dare to touch a mere human garment in this way, how would he dare to touch the body of the God who is over all, the blameless and pure one, to be in union with the divine nature which is the cause of our being and life, by which the gates of death were destroyed and taken up into the vault of heaven. How can we receive this with such great arrogance?

— ST. JOHN CHRYSOSTOM

PRAYER BEFORE MASS
Thomas à Kempis

✠ Lord, all things in heaven and earth are yours.
I desire to offer myself to you in free and perpetual oblation,
so that I may forever be with you.

Lord, in simplicity of heart, I offer
myself this day to you,
to be your servant in service and sacrifice
of perpetual praise.
Accept me with the oblation of your precious body,
which this day I offer you in the presence of your holy

The Eucharist — Source of an Apologist's Strength

angels, here invisibly present, so that it may be to my
salvation and to the salvation of all people.

TRADITIONAL PRAYER TO ANGELS AND SAINTS BEFORE MASS

✠ Angels, Archangels, Thrones, Dominations,
Principalities, Powers, celestial Virtues,
Cherubim and Seraphim;
all saints of God, holy men and women, and you
especially, my patrons:
deign to plead for me that I may have grace to offer
worthily this sacrifice
to almighty God, to the praise and glory of his name,
for my own welfare also and that of
all his holy Church.

PRAYER AFTER MASS TO THE BLESSED TRINITY
St. Thomas Aquinas

✠ May the tribute of my humble ministry be pleasing
to you, Holy Trinity.
Grant that the sacrifice which I—
as unworthy as I am—
have offered in the presence of your majesty, may
be acceptable to you.

Through your mercy may it bring forgiveness to me
and to all for whom I have offered it, through
Jesus Christ our Lord.

Humbly I implore thee,
let not this holy communion be to me an increase of
guilt unto my punishment,
but an availing plea unto pardon and salvation.
Let it be to me the armor of faith and the
shield of goodwill.

May it root out from my heart all vice;
may it utterly subdue my evil passions and
all my unruly desires.
May it perfect me in charity and patience,
in humility and obedience, and in all other virtues.

May it be my sure defense against the snares
laid for me by my enemies, visible and invisible.
May it restrain and quiet all my evil impulses,
and make me ever cleave to thee who
art the one true God.
May I owe to it a happy ending of my life.

The Eucharist is the principal power source of all an apologist's works. Another indispensable one is the Holy Bible, where the Word of God also makes his presence. Ignorance of Scripture

Sacred Scripture and the Holy Rosary

is ignorance of Christ, as St. Jerome famously advises. This means that knowledge of Scripture is knowledge of Christ, and time spent in Scripture's pages is time spent with the Lord. That the Catholic Church is the human author, compiler, guarantor, guardian, steward, and wielder of God's written word is another sign and cause of its holiness.

> Indeed, the word of God is living and effective, sharper than any two-edged sword, penetrating even between soul and spirit, joints and marrow, and able to discern reflections and thoughts of the heart.
>
> — HEBREWS 4:12

> If anyone ponders over the prophetic sayings . . . it is certain that in the very act of reading and diligently studying them his mind and feelings will be touched by a divine breath and he will recognize that the words he is reading are not the utterances of men but the language of God.
>
> — ORIGEN

One way to make Scripture come alive, and also take on a tactile reality, is praying the *rosary*.

> The rosary is a long chain that links heaven and earth. One end of it is in our hands and the other end is in the hands of the holy virgin.
>
> — ST. THÉRÈSE OF LISIEUX

The rosary is an incarnational prayer. It engages the senses: a visible crucifix, beads for the fingers, the rhythm of the oral prayers. It is both the premier Marian prayer, given to St. Dominic by our lady herself. And it is a meditative catechism on the life of the Lord. It is made for the daily reality of human lives: it can be prayed privately or publicly; while kneeling in a pew or sitting in a living room or walking through the forest or along a crowded city block. It is keyed to the days of the week and the weeks of the Church's calendar. Its mysteries begin, as the Gospel does, with Mary's yes to God's plan of redemption, just as our calendar year begins with the Solemnity of Mary, Mother of God.

And the rosary ends with Mary's coronation in heaven, reminding us of the glorious destiny that God has planned for each of us. One reason why apologetics is so important and so relevant is that the Faith traces for us a continuous trajectory between this life and the next. What is important to us now will be important to us forever; what we do and say and love today will help determine what we do forever. We who are members of a holy Church must pay attention to our hearts' desires, because our desires determine our priorities, and our time will eventually give way to our eternity.

> You have granted him his heart's desire;
> you did not refuse the request of his lips.
>
> — PSALM 21:3

> Delight yourself in the Lord,
> and he will give you the desires of your heart.
>
> — PSALM 37:4

Sacred Scripture and the Holy Rosary

For where your treasure is,
there your heart will be also.

— MATTHEW 6:21

Father, if you are willing, take this cup away from me; still, not my will but yours be done.

— LUKE 22:42

God has desires for his creatures; for instance, he "wills everyone to be saved and to come to knowledge of the truth" (1 Tim. 2:4). Yet he also allows creatures to have desires for their own lives. In the heart of fallen man, these two sets of desires often disagree. Our hearts need a lifetime of healing, by God's grace, to align with his heart better. Yet God clearly prefers free persons over puppets.

PRAYER TO GOD OUR TRUE REST
Thomas à Kempis

✠ O most merciful Lord, grant to me thy grace,
   that it may be with me,
   and labor with me, and persevere with
   me even to the end.
   Grant that I may always desire and will
   that which is to you most acceptable, and most dear.
   Let thy will be mine, and my will ever follow yours,
   and agree perfectly with it.

> Grant to me, above all things that can be
> desired, to rest in you,
> and in you to have my heart at peace.
> You are the true peace of the heart, our only rest;
> apart from you, all things are hard and restless.
> In this very peace, that is, in you, the one chief
> eternal good, I will sleep and rest.

We must be careful, though, to reject the conclusion that our human desire is in itself wrong—in itself always an impediment to holiness. This kind of quasi-Buddhism rejects Christian truth about how God made us. We are not drones but individuals, whom God created and whom he loves in our particularity—including the desires of our heart. Becoming a saint means not destroying those desires, but freeing and perfecting them. We become "man fully alive" as in St. Irenaeus's famous phrase: more aligned with God's will and his truth and yet also more perfectly ourselves in our individuality.

Unlike angels, we occupy particular places and times. We are in relationship with particular other humans in those times and places; there are anniversaries to remember, shared experiences to treasure, a thousand small associations that sweeten life's tiny moments and mark us in our unique particularity. And these things *matter*. This is the Church, Christ's mystical body on earth, and for its holiness the Son of God took all of humanity—and every little individual thing that is human—to himself.

PRAYER TO THE SACRED HEART OF JESUS

✠ Most sacred, most loving heart of Jesus,
you are concealed in the holy Eucharist, and
you bear for us still.
Now, as then, you say: "With desire I have desired."
I worship you with all my best love and awe,
with fervent affection,
with my most subdued, most resolved will.

For a while you take up your abode within me.
O make my heart beat with your heart!
Purify it of all that is earthly, all that
is proud and sensual,
of all perversity, of all disorder.

Fill it with you, such that neither
the events of the day
nor the circumstance of the time may have the
power to ruffle it;
but that in your love and your fear, it may have peace.

Catholicity

The word *Catholic* is derived from two Greek words meaning "according to" (*kata*) "the whole" (*holos*); it is most simply commonly translated as "universal." The Church is not named for a human founder (e.g., Lutheran) or for its a location (e.g., Fifth Street Baptist) or a theological movement (e.g., Reformed). Rather, it took on a name, organically and within the first century of its founding, that signifies its embrace of all humanity. The name *Catholic* captures God's desire for his entire creation and all in it to be his. Sin divides us interiorly and pits us against others, but the grace that flows through Christ's universal Church heals and unites us.

To make us fully integrated persons and to unify the human race, at the moment of the Annunciation God regathers all of humanity in the new Eve, so that she may present each and all to the new Adam. In the universal Church, we are one body reunited under Christ's singular headship.

> It is called Catholic then because it extends over all the world, from one end of the earth to the other; and because it teaches universally and completely one and all the doctrines which ought to come to men's knowledge, concerning things both visible and invisible, heavenly and earthly; and because it brings into subjection to godliness the whole race of mankind, governors and governed, learned and unlearned; and because it universally treats and heals the whole class of sins, which are committed by soul or body, and possesses in itself every form of virtue which is named, both in deeds and words, and in every kind of spiritual gifts.
>
> — ST. CYRIL OF JERUSALEM

A Universal Church and an Enduring Doctrine

The young Augustine of Hippo defied the Church's Catholicity when he fell in with a quasi-Christian sect called the *Manicheans*, so-called after their third-century Persian mystic founder Mani. When he had later become a Catholic and a bishop, looking back on the foolishness of his youth, Augustine wrote against the Manicheans, using his past wanderings as a warning to help others find their way to their true home on earth. He opens by admitting that the wisdom of the Church is one of his main attractions to living as a Catholic, but

> The consent of peoples and nations keeps me in the Church; so does her authority, inaugurated by miracles, nourished by hope, enlarged by love, established by age. The succession of priests keeps me, beginning from the very seat of the apostle Peter, to whom the Lord, after his resurrection, gave it in charge to feed his sheep, down to the present episcopate. And so, lastly, does the name itself of Catholic, which, not without reason, amid so many heresies, the Church has thus retained; so that, though all heretics wish to be called Catholics, yet when a stranger asks where the Catholic Church meets, no heretic will venture to point to his own chapel or house . . . For my part, I should not believe the gospel except as moved by the authority of the Catholic Church.
>
> — ST. AUGUSTINE

It is the universal acknowledgment that this is the lone Church that claims to have been founded by Jesus himself and built upon the rock of St. Peter. Its unbroken succession of authority from apostles and its continuity of beliefs and practices made Augustine unable to imagine a spiritual life outside of its walls. And likewise does that mark of catholicity compel so many believers and seekers to this day.

PRAYER FOR THE CHURCH

✠ We pray you, O almighty and eternal God!
Who through Jesus Christ has revealed your
glory to all nations,
to preserve the works of your mercy,
that your Church, being spread
through the whole world,
may continue with unchanging faith in the
confession of your name.

An unchanging Faith for all the nations. This is the mark of catholicity that points to the true Church—intended for all people, for all time, and in every circumstance and walk of life. Here the famous formula of Vincent of Lérins (d. 445) serves as both a meditation on catholicity an apologetical tool for identifying Catholic truth and the proper development thereof. Namely, that it must bear the signs of *universality, antiquity,* and *consent.*

A Universal Church and an Enduring Doctrine

> Moreover, in the Catholic Church itself, all possible care must be taken, that we hold that faith which has been believed everywhere, always, by all. For that is truly and in the strictest sense Catholic, which, as the name itself and the reason of the thing declare, comprehends all universally. This rule we shall observe if we follow universality, antiquity, consent. We shall follow universality if we confess that one faith to be true, which the whole Church throughout the world confesses; antiquity, if we in no wise depart from those interpretations which it is manifest were notoriously held by our holy ancestors and fathers; consent, in like manner, if in antiquity itself we adhere to the consentient definitions and determinations of all, or at the least of almost all priests and doctors.
>
> — ST. VINCENT OF LÉRINS

The Catholic Church is not a democracy! It is no merely human organization rocked by the inevitable sea changes of popular opinion. It is a divine, mystical, living body: countless branches grafted onto the one true Vine. Its true branches and fruitful growth are therefore secured by that which is held *quod ubique*, everywhere; *semper*, always; and *ab omnibus*, by all. That is what to be Catholic means: to draw life from the one vine together.

PRAYER FOR UNITY
Dionysius of the Syrian Jacobite Church

✠ O God the Father, origin of divinity, good
beyond all that is good,
fair beyond all that is fair, in whom is calmness,
peace, and concord;
you who make up the dissensions that divide
us from each other,
and bring us back into a unity of love,
which may bear some likeness to thy divine nature.

And as you are above all things,
make us one by the unanimity of a good mind,
that through the embrace of charity and the
bonds of affection,
we may be spiritually one, as well in
ourselves as in each other;
through that peace of yours which makes
all things peaceful,
and through the grace, mercy, and tenderness of
thy Son, Jesus Christ.

Apostolicity

Every Christian is called to be *apostolic* in his own life—that is, to be one who understands that we are on a mission, that we have been sent (Greek, *stole*) out (*apo*) to bring the good news of Jesus Christ to those providentially placed in our life. Our "careers" may come and go but our vocation is ultimately baptismal—the life God has given us to continue and thus communicate his life to others—and it lasts our whole life.

> We, the ordinary people of the streets, believe with all our might that this street, that this world where God has placed us, is, for us, the site of our holiness.
>
> —VEN. MADELEINE DELBRÊL

The Catholic Church is *apostolic* because it is founded on the apostles, to whom the Lord Jesus entrusted the deposit of Christian faith and the authority to teach, govern, and sanctify in his name. The mark of apostolicity includes not only that founding but the visible continuity of belief, authority, and worship from the apostles to today.

> You are the eternal Shepherd who never leaves his flock untended. Through the apostles you watch over us and protect us always. You made them shepherds of the flock to share in the work of your Son.
>
> — *ROMAN MISSAL*, PREFACE I OF THE APOSTLES

Traditionally, the Church has identified certain kinds of apostolic actions that all the faithful can perform, and thus embody the mark of apostolicity. These are the *seven corporal works of mercy* and the *seven spiritual works of mercy*. Through these, we imitate the apostles in imitating Christ, who perfectly modeled how to love and serve our neighbor, body and soul. These works come mainly from the Lord's Sermon on the Mount and from his admonitions in Matthew 25, as well as from Isaiah and the book of Tobit.

The Corporal Works of Mercy

1. Feed the hungry (Matt. 25:35)

2. Give drink to the thirsty (Matt. 25:35)

3. Clothe the naked (Matt. 25:36)

4. Visit the imprisoned (Matt. 25:36)

5. Shelter the homeless (Matt. 25:35)

6. Visit the sick (Matt. 25:36)

7. Bury the dead (Tob. 1:17–19, 12:12–14)

The Spiritual Works of Mercy

1. To instruct the ignorant (Matt. 28:19–20; John 20:21)

Apologetics is an Apostolic Work

2. To counsel the doubtful (John 14:27)

3. To admonish sinners (Luke 15:7–10)

4. To bear wrongs patiently (Luke 6:27–31)

5. To forgive offenses willingly (Matt. 6:12)

6. To comfort the afflicted (Matt. 11:28)

7. To pray for the living and the dead (John 17:24)

PRAYER FOR JUSTICE
Fr. John A. Hardon, S.J.

✠ Lord Jesus, carpenter and king, supreme sovereign of all men,
look with tender mercy upon the multitudes of our day
who bear the indignities of injustice everywhere.
Raise up leaders in every land dedicated to your standards of order, equity, and justice.
Grant unto us, Lord Jesus, the grace to be worthy members of your mystical body,
laboring unceasingly to fulfil our vocation in the social apostolate of your Church.

> Sharpen our intellects to pierce the
> pettiness of prejudice;
> to perceive the beauty of true human brotherhood.
> Guide our minds to a meaningful understanding of
> the problems of the poor,
> of the oppressed, of the unemployed, of all in need of
> assistance anywhere.
> Guide our hearts against the subtle
> lure of earthly things
> and undue regard for those who possess them.
> May we hunger and thirst after justice always.

The Church has always rooted its apostolic work in the world in its faith and worship—the reason for and the sustainer of that work. In recent times, however, some have sought to separate the Church's social action from its doctrine, morals, and liturgy. However well-intended in some cases, this approach rejects the mark of apostolicity, reducing the Church's mission to the labors of just one more social work agency, one more non-profit in the world. The Lord came, and founded the apostolic Church, to do infinitely more than that. That is why the best of the Church's social mission finds its origin and ultimate end in the Eucharist.

> Do you want to honor Christ's body? Then do not scorn him in his nakedness, nor honor him here in the Church with silken garments while neglecting him outside where he is cold and naked. For he who said: This is my body, and made it

Apologetics is an Apostolic Work

> so by his words, also said: you *saw me hungry and did not feed me, and inasmuch as you did not do it for one of these, the least of my brothers or sisters, you did not do it for me* . . . Do not, therefore, adorn the Church and ignore your afflicted brother, for he is the most precious temple of all.
>
> — ST. JOHN CHRYSOSTOM

When we work to alleviate our neighbors' sufferings—whether spiritual or physical—we are in fact tending, *ministering*, to Christ, whom it pleased to identify with their lowliness and take it to himself. This is the work of an apostle.

> Therefore, as we celebrate the memorial of his death and resurrection,
> we offer you, Lord, the bread of life and the chalice of salvation,
> giving thanks that you have held us worthy to be in your presence and minister to you.
>
> — *ROMAN MISSAL*, SECOND EUCHARISTIC PRAYER

Uniting us to the graces of the cross through the Church's liturgy, Christ not only bears our infirmities and crosses but empowers us to bring his love and healing presence to others. Since we make up the Savior's body and bear his presence in our souls, our sufferings become salvific—not in and of themselves, of course, but as continuations of Calvary. And, in the beautiful economy of salvation, our prayers and privations also can benefit our brothers and sisters in purgatory—carrying the Church's apostolic mission even beyond death, to the very gates of heaven.

> It is therefore a holy and wholesome thought to pray for the dead, that they may be loosed from sins.
>
> — 2 MACCABEES 12:46, DOUAY-RHEIMS

HEROIC ACT OF CHARITY

✠ Heavenly Father, in union with the
merits of Jesus and Mary,
I offer to you for the sake of the poor souls
all the satisfactory value of my works during life,
as well as all that will be done for me after death.
I give you my all through the hands of the
Immaculate Virgin Mary
that she may set free whatever souls she pleases,
according to her heavenly wisdom and
mother's love for them.
Receive this offering, O God, and grant me in return
an increase of your grace.

The Four Last Things

ETERNAL REST

✠ Eternal rest grant unto them, O Lord,
And let perpetual light shine upon them.
May they rest in peace.

Our mortal passing from this world occasions what the Church calls the *four last things*: death, judgment, hell, and heaven. It is fitting to conclude our spiritual reflections with this subject, as these last things in our lives are also often the *first* things in the order of apologetics and evangelization. For the Faith is infinitely more than a self-help handbook or a cheat code for a happy life. It is the guiding star by which we set course, and the vessel in which we journey, to the destination for which we were all created and thus we universally desire: the bliss of eternal life.

Why Jesus? Why Catholicism? Because we all wish for a happy ending. At the same time, we all perceive, as G.K. Chesterton observed, that "we are in a net of sin." The beginning of conversion, right now—for each of us in daily walk with God and for those to whom we witness—is a resolve to influence our last things, to write a happy ending.

> Let me receive pure light; when I shall have arrived there, then shall I be a man.
>
> — ST. IGNATIUS OF ANTIOCH

Death is the result of humanity's primal disobedience. Mankind was brought into existence to be a living unity of body and soul; but death robs us of our integrated glory, dividing us, for a time, into our composite parts—removing our soul from the sphere of this world while our body remains (yet, imagine a creature who would be immaculately conceived without sin and how that person would not have to undergo this unnatural separation and would thus not have to wait for the reunion of *her* body and soul—i.e., see how the Dogmas of the Immaculate Conception and the Assumption are rational and related).

> The souls of the righteous are in the hand of God, and no torment shall touch them. They seemed, in the view of the foolish, to be dead; and their passing away was thought an affliction and their going forth from us, utter destruction. But they are in peace. For if to others, indeed, they seem punished, yet is their hope full of immortality; chastised a little, they shall be greatly blessed, because God tried them and found them worthy of himself.
>
> — WISDOM 3:1–5

The Blessed Mother, who was preveniently preserved from original sin by Christ's redemptive grace, did not have to undergo this unnatural separation but rather fell asleep in this world and was assumed, body and soul united, into the next. We can look forward to that same destiny, if not the same way of arriving there: for the resurrected Christ has transformed death for all of us, too, turning the sorrow of our earthly end into a heavenly transformation, a doorway to endless joy.

> Because of Christ, Christian death has a positive meaning: "For to me to live is Christ, and to die is

gain" (Phil. 1:21). "The saying is sure: if we have died with him, we will also live with him" (2 Tim. 2:11). What is essentially new about Christian death is this: through baptism, the Christian has already "died with Christ" sacramentally, in order to live a new life; and if we die in Christ's grace, physical death completes this "dying with Christ" and so completes our incorporation into him in his redeeming act.

— CATECHISM OF THE CATHOLIC CHURCH

From the cross, Jesus entrusted his mother to his beloved apostle, John. Pious tradition has always held to the opinion that this entrustment happened because St. Joseph had already passed, surrounded at that moment by Jesus and Mary and thus forever after the *patron saint of a happy death*.

PRAYER TO ST. JOSEPH
From Pope Julius II to Emperor Charles V

✠ O, St. Joseph, whose protection is so great, so strong, so prompt before the throne of God, I place in you all of my interests and desires. Oh, St. Joseph, do assist me by your powerful intercession, and obtain for me from your divine Son all spiritual blessings, through him, Jesus Christ our Lord. I ask this so that, having engaged here below your heavenly power, I may offer thanksgiving and homage to the most loving of Fathers.

O, St. Joseph, I never weary of contemplating you, and the child Jesus asleep in your arms. I dare not approach while he is asleep near your heart. Press him in my name and kiss his beautiful head for me and ask him to return the kiss when I draw my dying breath. St. Joseph, patron of departing souls, pray for me.

The second last thing is our personal *judgment*. After the soul's final separation from the body, each of us will be judged by the Creator according to our life's words, works, and omissions.

> At the evening of life, we shall be judged on our love.
> — ST. JOHN OF THE CROSS

This *particular judgment* is different from the *final* and universal judgment of all, which will occur at the end of time when all the dead are resurrected and the doors to heaven and hell are finally sealed. These two judgments are not in opposition, but they differ according to the time and manner in which they occur.

Soon I will stand before the ultimate judge of my life. Although in looking back on my long life I may have much cause for fear and dread, I have nevertheless a joyful spirit because I firmly trust

> that the Lord is not only the righteous judge, but, at the same time, the friend and brother who has already suffered my inadequacies himself and therefore, as judge, is at the same time my advocate. Looking at the hour of judgment, the grace of being a Christian thus becomes clear to me. Being a Christian gives me knowledge and, moreover, friendship with the judge of my life, and enables me to cross the dark door of death with confidence.
>
> — POPE BENEDICT XVI

God's just judgment, which we deserve and which none can evade, is not incompatible with the divine love that is the soul of apologetics and the hope (1 Pet. 3:15) that apologists and evangelists offer the world. We must understand, and emphasize when we witness to the Faith, that God's love is perfect but it isn't "safe." It is not a reflection of modern "tolerance"—sappy, sentimental, and weak—but a consuming fire.

> "Now if any one builds on the foundation with gold, silver, precious stones, wood, hay, straw—each man's work will become manifest; for the day will disclose it, because it will be revealed with fire, and the fire will test what sort of work each one has done. If the work which any man has built on the foundation survives, he will receive a reward. If any man's work is burned up, he will suffer loss, though he himself will be saved, but only as through fire" (1 Cor. 3:12–15) . . . in order to be saved we personally have to pass through "fire" so as to

become fully open to receiving God and able to take our place at the table of the eternal marriage-feast.

Some recent theologians are of the opinion that the fire which both burns and saves is Christ himself, the judge and Savior. The encounter with him is the decisive act of judgment. Before his gaze all falsehood melts away. This encounter with him, as it burns us, transforms and frees us, allowing us to become truly ourselves. All that we build during our lives can prove to be mere straw, pure bluster, and it collapses.

— POPE BENEDICT XVI

We only live, only suspire
Consumed by either fire or fire.

— T.S. ELIOT, *THE FOUR QUARTETS*

Although other accounts vary, Maisie Ward reports that G.K. Chesterton's dying words were, "The issue is now clear. It is between light and darkness and every one must choose his side." Perhaps the doors to hell have only one handle and it faces each of us; in the end, perhaps God does not "send" anyone to hell. Instead it may be we—in perhaps the greatest of contradictions and mysteries of iniquity—choose to go through and slam that infernal door behind us forever.

The Four Last Things

> Better to reign in hell than serve in heaven.
>
> — JOHN MILTON, *PARADISE LOST*

Since God wants to make us free lovers, not programmed drones, *hell* is a necessary corollary of free will. It is the crystallization of the paradox of sin: we choose what we know will not bring us final happiness, because in the moment we prefer to it the temporary satisfaction of having our own way. What else was the sin of Adam and Eve?

Scripture is quite clear that each person makes this definitive choice according to how he lives—the totality of his life's moral choices. Damnation is often depicted with images of God's wrath; but is we who, by our disobedience, first signify our rejection of him. This is the patristic concept of *aversio ad Deo*—the turning-away from God—as the root of all sin.

> Many of those who sleep in the dust of the earth shall awake; some to everlasting life; others to reproach and everlasting disgrace.
>
> — DANIEL 12:2

> For see, the Lord will come in fire, his chariots like the stormwind; to wreak his anger in burning rage and his rebuke in fiery flames.
>
> — ISAIAH 66:15

> By your stubbornness and impenitent heart, you are storing up wrath for yourself for the day of

> wrath and revelation of the just judgment of God, who will repay everyone according to his works: eternal life to those who seek glory, honor, and immortality through perseverance in good works, but wrath and fury to those who selfishly disobey the truth and obey wickedness. Yes, affliction and distress will come upon every human being who does evil, Jew first and then Greek.
>
> — ROMANS 2:5–9

> Then they will answer and say, "Lord, when did we see you hungry or thirsty or a stranger or naked or ill or in prison, and not minister to your needs?" He will answer them, "Amen, I say to you, what you did not do for one of these least ones, you did not do for me." And these will go off to eternal punishment, but the righteous to eternal life.
>
> — MATTHEW 25:44–46

Apologists who explain the four last things often get asked if we can pray for those already in hell. Though this seems like an act of love and mercy, since it amounts to asking God to override their free will and undo what they insisted be done, it is really more like blasphemy than love. Yet we *can* pray for ourselves and our neighbors—we whose future is not written, who have the option of turning *toward* God, *conversio ad Deo,* before us with every choice, every cooperation with grace, that we make. We pray for *final perseverance*: that until the end of our lives we may be open to the graces of salvation—probably not perfect, but always repentant—rejecting the empty promises of Satan that are ultimately the empty promises of self-worship.

PRAYER TO BANISH THE FORCES OF EVIL

✠ Spirit of our God, Father, Son and Holy
Spirit, most Holy Trinity,
Immaculate Virgin Mary, angels, archangels, and
saints of heaven, descend upon me.
Please purify me, Lord, mold me, fill me
with yourself, use me.
Banish all the forces of evil from me,
destroy them, defeat them,
so that I can be healthy and do good deeds.

Banish from me all spells, witchcraft, black magic,
evil spells, ties, and curses;
all diabolic infestations, oppressions, possessions;
all ailments physical, psychological, moral,
spiritual, and diabolical;
all that is evil and sinful.

Burn all these evils in hell,
that they may never again touch me
or any other creature in the entire world.
I command and bid all the powers that molest me—
by the power of God all-powerful, in the name of

THE SOUL OF APOLOGETICS

> Jesus Christ our Savior,
> through the intercession of the
> Immaculate Virgin Mary—
> to leave me forever, and to be consigned into the
> everlasting hell where they will be bound
> by St. Michael the archangel, St. Gabriel, St. Raphael,
> our guardian angels,
> and where they will be crushed under the heel of the
> Immaculate Virgin Mary.

Scripture and the Catholic tradition have offered every form of imagery, song, poetry, and promise to depict *heaven*. The truth is, however, that the experience of the beatific vision—our free union with the inexhaustible love of God—must transcend any attempt of ours to describe it! What we *can* know is that heaven is less *residential* than it is *relational*, more of a person than a place. Heaven is the perfection of life in Christ, our perfect and eternal transformation into a child of the Father, and the joy and brilliance of bearing within us, as his temple, the Holy Spirit. All while surrounded by the saints in loving communion.

> This perfect life with the most Holy Trinity—this communion of life and love with the Trinity, with the Virgin Mary, the angels and all the blessed— is called "heaven." Heaven is the ultimate end and fulfillment of the deepest human longings, the state of supreme, definitive happiness.
>
> — *CATECHISM OF THE CATHOLIC CHURCH*

Accordingly, we "celebrate" Masses for the dead because we desire such communion, such relationship, for our brothers and sisters. And we have inexhaustible trust that God is more faithful than we are fickle; that heaven is a sign of God's fidelity more than our own. Heaven is so far beyond what we could ever merit or demand, even when we do cooperate with God's grace and spend a life turning toward him, that it is best understood as the fulfillment of what we received at baptism—God's totally free gift of self.

PRAYER OF COMMENDATION NEAR THE TIME OF DEATH

✠ Go forth, Christian soul, from this world
in the name of God the almighty
Father, who created you,
in the name of Jesus Christ, Son of the living God,
who suffered for you,
in the name of the Holy Spirit, who was
poured out upon you.

Go forth, faithful Christian.
May you live in peace this day;
may your home be with God in Zion,
with Mary, the virgin mother of God,
with Joseph, and all the angels and saints.

THE SOUL OF APOLOGETICS

PRAYER UPON THE TIME OF DEATH

✠ In your hands, O Lord, we humbly entrust
our brother (sister).
In this life you embraced him (her)
with your tender love;
deliver him (her) now from every evil and bid
him (her) eternal rest.

The old order has passed away:
welcome our brother/sister into paradise,
where there will be no sorrow, no weeping or pain,
but fullness of peace and joy
with your Son and the Holy Spirit forever and ever.

CONCLUSION

The Soul of Apologetics

Let us close this volume where we began, with the theme that is both the soul of apologetics and the one judge of our lives on earth: love.

The soul of apologetics is love because above all it is a work of love. We engage others with the truths of Christ and his Church because we wish to imitate the Lord in loving them and to assist the Lord in saving their souls.

This is what St. Paul means when he exhorts us all to have "the same attitude that is also yours in Christ Jesus" (Phil. 2:5). This "attitude" or *phronesis* in Paul's Greek is the term for an other-worldly practical wisdom, a type of brilliance that combines both our intellectual abilities and the manner of our living. Apologetics means acting like Christ in order to build up the body of Christ through love. It is, as Paul continues, about emptying ourselves (Phil. 2:6–11) in order to gain souls for that mystical body.

This foundational apostle—Paul, who went to the intellectual, cultural, and social peripheries of Christ's early

Church—consistently instructs that we should all be "living the truth in love" and that "we should grow in every way into him who is the head, Christ, from whom the whole body, joined and held together by every supporting ligament, with the proper functioning of each part, brings about the body's growth and builds itself up in love" (Eph. 4:15–16).

For though it is true that love can only "rejoice with the truth" (1 Cor. 13:6), the converse is also true: the truth can rejoice only in love. When, instead, truth and love are separated and siloed, the spirit of evil has an opening to exploit our pride. And then, no matter how airtight our logic or how thorough our command of the facts, and no matter how beautiful and attractive the Catholic faith is, arrogance and anger can rob our work of its merit and its end.

No one has ever been argued into holiness, but all the saints have been *loved* into holiness. And since we cannot love what we do not know, and we cannot know a God who has revealed himself as Love without loving him and all that he has revealed, our work of apologetics must always aim to unite truth and charity, reason and faith, the head and the heart. And this can be done only through a deep and profound union with Jesus Christ. For if it does not proceed from Jesus' sanctifying presence in our souls, everything we do will be but dross.

When, however, we are made by grace who Jesus is by nature, his gaze becomes ours, and the way he interacts with others is taken up into our own thoughts, words, and actions. Our lives are made godly; every instance of our existence becomes more and more integrated with the One for whom we have been created. When this happens, our manner of being and speaking with others is deified into an inseparable bond of charity. It becomes, in St. Augustine's phrase, "knowledge together with love." He goes on to describe a state that equally serves

The Inseparability of Love and Truth

to characterize the aim or the apologist: one in which "both the word is in love and love is in the word, and both are in him who loves and speaks."

> Yet I live, no longer I, but Christ lives in me.
>
> — GALATIANS 2:20

Love forms a connatural bond between the lover and the beloved. As kinship grows between creature and Creator, it directs us to its perfection and personification in the Logos, the Word in Love: Jesus Christ.

Does it not make a difference—*all* the difference—to know that this world is the product of a self-giving God who creates, sustains all things in their being, and has ordered all things to the most loving of destinies rather than the chance result of some cosmic conflagration, the origin of which cannot be explained and for which there can be no real purpose or end? To defend the Faith, then, is ultimately to proclaim that the universe is a meaningful place: that all things bear the mark of God's Word, who enlightens our intellects and empowers us to see all reality in its defining light.

Likewise, as the Lord lives in us and we become more like him, we embrace others as brother and sister. This fraternity that makes human relationships beautiful and blessed is the antidote to the modern madness of exploitation and alienation. To defend the Faith of the God who became one of us is to promote the universal bond of charity among men: the human accord that so many false philosophies, willfully rejecting the divine principle of fraternity, claim to seek but fail to achieve.

Sometimes those philosophies crib from Christian truth. They claim love or even "God's love" for themselves. But since love is inseparable from truth, simply crying "love, love" does not by itself bring us closer either to love's source or its ends. If God as love and we as lovers differ so vastly that what "love" is to us means nothing to God; if God's love and our "love" do not meet, do not overlap, do not cohere in truth, we remain forever in the dark about what love really is.

> If God's moral judgments differ from ours so that our "black" may be his "white," we can mean nothing by calling him good; for to say "God is good," while asserting that his goodness is wholly other than ours, is really only to say "God is we know not what." An utterly unknown quality in God cannot give us moral grounds for loving or obeying him. If he is not (in our sense) "good" we shall obey, if at all, only through fear—and should be equally ready to obey an omnipotent Fiend.
>
> — C.S. LEWIS

Deep down, everyone made in God's image and likeness senses what true love is; every one of us has an idea and a taste of perfect self-gift, of perfect charity. Philosophers have called this the "natural desire for God"—the germ that must be fostered and grown in the soul of every imperfect being naturally desiring perfection. This desire grows in our souls through the graces of holy baptism and the other sacraments, and it blossoms in the soul of the apologist when we receive every interlocutor, every debate opponent, every truth-seeker placed in our path, with the selfless love of Jesus. Without it, our loves can't overlap.

The Inseparability of Love and Truth

Love remains just a concept, and the light of truth remains hidden in shadows.

> How much more boldly ought we to say that a man is drawn to Christ when he delights in the truth, when he delights in blessedness, delights in righteousness, delights in everlasting life, all which Christ is? ... Give me a man that loves, and he feels what I say. Give me one that longs, one that hungers, one that is traveling in this wilderness, and thirsting and panting after the fountain of his eternal home; give such, and he knows what I say.
>
> — ST. AUGUSTINE

If a man loves rightly, he loves Jesus; if a man rejoices in what is true, he rejoices in Christ; if a man delights in what is eternal, he glories in the Lord.

It can be a challenge in today's overwhelming culture of apathy—the ancient vice of *acedia*—to sense what we long for, what we hunger for, what the human heart truly desires. Nonetheless, we are hardwired for truth and union. To defend the Faith is thus to unlock that desire in others, and to present its fulfilment in a living Person—ever-merciful, perfectly loving, and entirely joy-filled—who is both the way to happiness and its end.

> All people feel the interior impulse to love authentically: love and truth never abandon them completely, because these are the vocation planted

by God in the heart and mind of every human person. The search for love and truth is purified and liberated by Jesus Christ from the impoverishment that our humanity brings to it, and he reveals to us in all its fullness the initiative of love and the plan for true life that God has prepared for us. In Christ, charity in truth becomes the Face of his Person, a vocation for us to love our brothers and sisters in the truth of his plan. Indeed, he himself is the Truth.

— POPE BENEDICT XVI

Truth and love are not abstract essences but are really just names for the Second Person of the Trinity, who, out of love for wayward humanity, took on mortal flesh and freely went to die in the most ignoble and inhumane way. To defend the Faith, then, is to make present the most lasting symbol for this overarching love: the pierced heart of the Savior.

The Sacred Heart—wholly God's initiative, gratuitous and unmerited—is our school of charity. It is the pedagogy of love for apologists. In it, love is nakedly visible, pierced through and offered to all. Such visibility invites us also to show our heart, to be vulnerable in our work of proclaiming truth and winning souls.

> Devotion to the Heart of Jesus has given form to the prophetic words recalled by St. John: "They shall look on him whom they have pierced" (John 19:37; cf. Zec. 12:10). It is a contemplative gaze, "which strives to enter deeply into the sentiments

The Inseparability of Love and Truth

of Christ, true God and true man. In this devotion the believer confirms and deepens the acceptance of the mystery of the Incarnation, which has made the Word one with human beings and thus given witness to the Father's search for them. This seeking is born in the intimate depths of God, who loves man eternally in the Word, and wishes to raise him in Christ to the dignity of an adoptive son" (*Tertio Millennio Adveniente*). At the same time, devotion to the Heart of Jesus searches the mystery of the Redemption in order to discover the measure of love, which prompted his sacrifice for our salvation.

— POPE ST. JOHN PAUL II

Gazing upon the traditional picture of Christ offering his heart with his pierced hands, we may pray never to fall into a sort of Pelagianism or Jansenism, wrongly thinking that my power to preach is entirely up to me and that everyone I engage is my responsibility to save. Defending and explaining the Faith is the Lord's work, in which it pleases him to cooperate with us. All we have to offer is what Jesus first opened himself up to give. We do not produce truth and grace; they come forth from the Father's Word and Christ's pierced side. This is the deepest and most central mystery, the magnificent divine power that sustains the soul of apologetics.

THE SOUL OF APOLOGETICS

CONSECRATION TO THE SACRED HEART OF JESUS
Pope St. John Paul II

✠ Lord Jesus Christ, Redeemer of the human race,
to your most Sacred Heart we turn
with humility and trust,
with reverence and hope, with a deep
desire to give to you
glory and honor and praise.
Lord Jesus Christ, Savior of the world,
we thank you for all that you are and all that you do.
Lord Jesus Christ, Son of the Living God,
we praise you for the love that you have revealed
through your Sacred Heart,
which was pierced for us and which has become the
fountain of our joy,
the source of our eternal life.
Gathered together in your Name,
which is above all other names,
we consecrate ourselves to your most Sacred Heart,
in which dwells the fullness of truth and charity.
In consecrating ourselves to you,
we faithful renew our desire to respond in love
to the rich outpouring of your merciful love.
Lord Jesus Christ, King of love and Prince of peace,

The Inseparability of Love and Truth

reign in our hearts and in our homes.
Conquer all the powers of evil
and bring us to share in the victory
of your Sacred Heart.
May all we say and do give glory and praise to you
and to the Father and the Holy Spirit,
one God living and reigning for ever and ever.

AMEN

Works Cited in this Book

Catechism of the Catholic Church

The *Didache*

Odes of Solomon

St. Ambrose, Commentary on Luke

St. Amphilocius of Iconium, *On the Hypapante*

St. Augustine, *Against the Fundamental Epistle of Mani*

St. Augustine, *Commentary on the Psalms*

St. Augustine, *Confessions*

St. Augustine, *The Literal Meaning of Genesis*

St. Augustine, *On Christian Doctrine*

St. Augustine, *On Genesis: A Refutation Against the Manichees*

St. Augustine, *On the Trinity*

St. Basil the Great, *On the Holy Spirit*

St. Benedict of Nursia, *The Rule*

Blaise Pascal, *Pensées*

St. Bonaventure, *Itinerarium*

Charles Williams, *The Figure of Beatrice*

C.S. Lewis, *The Four Loves*

C.S. Lewis, *Mere Christianity*

C.S. Lewis, *Poems*

St. Cyprian of Carthage, *On the Unity of the Church*

St. Cyril of Alexandria, *Third Letter to Nestorius*

St. Cyril of Jerusalem, *Catechetical Lecture*

Dante, *The Divine Comedy*

St. Diadochus of Photike, *Gnostic Chapters*

Edith Stein, "Love of the Cross"

Frank Sheed, *Christ in Eclipse*

Gerard Manley Hopkins, "God's Grandeur"

G.K. Chesterton, *A Miscellany of Men*

G.K. Chesterton, *Orthodoxy*

Works Cited

St. Gregory of Nyssa, *Commentary on the Song of Songs*

St. Gregory the Wonderworker, *Homily Concerning the Holy Mother of God Ever-Virgin*

Hans Urs von Balthasar, *Glory of the Lord*

Henri de Lubac, *Catholicism*

St. Ignatius of Antioch, *Epistle to the Smyrnaeans*

St. Ignatius of Loyola, *Spiritual Exercises*

St. Irenaeus of Lyons, *Against Heresies*

Jean Cardinal Daniélou, *Spiritual Diary*

St. Jerome, *Epistle 22*

St. Jerome, *Prologue to the Commentary on Isaiah*

St. John Chrysostom, *The Cemetery and the Cross*

St. John Chrysostom, *Homily on 1 Corinthians*

St. John Chrysostom, *Homily on Matthew*

St. John Henry Newman, *Lectures on the Present Position of Catholics in England*

St. John Henry Newman, *Parochial Sermons*

St. John Henry Newman, *Meditations on Christian Doctrine*

John Milton, *Paradise Lost*

St. John of the Cross, *Dichos*

St. Justin Martyr, *Dialogue With Trypho*

St. Maximus the Confessor, *Theological and Economic Chapters*

Origen, *On First Principles*

Pope Benedict XVI, *Spe Salvi*

Pope St. John Paul II, *Address to High School Students*

Pope St. John Paul II, *General Audience, March 10, 1999*

Pope Leo I, *Sermon on the Birth of Our Lord*

Pope Leo I, *The Tome*

Tertullian, *On Prayer*

St. Thomas Aquinas, *Summa Theologiae*

St. Thomas Aquinas, *Commentary on Romans*

St. Vincent of Lerins, *Commonitory*

Prayer Index

Act of Charity, *137*

Act of Consecration to Mary, *101*

Act of Contrition, *74*

Act of Faith, *136*

Act of Hope, *136*

After Holy Communion, *159*

After Mass to the Blessed Trinity, *165*

Against Temptation, *125*

Ancient Latin Prayer at the *Orate, Fratres*, *55*

Banish the Forces of Evil, *191*

Be Born in Us, Incarnate Love, *83*

Be Kind to Your Children, *147*

Before Mass, *164*

Come, Holy Spirit, *131*

Commendation Near the Time of Death, *193*

Consecration to the Sacred Heart of Jesus, *202*

Deliverance from Evil, *24, 69*

Eternal Rest, *183*

For Awareness of God's Presence in Every Moment, *110*

For the Church, *174*

God Our Refuge and Our Strength, *145*

God Our True Rest, *169*

Heroic Act of Charity, *182*

Humbly Beg God's Grace, *157*

Invocation of the Blessed Mother, *103*

Justice, *179*

Memorare, *108*

Morning Prayer of St. Basil the Great, *115*

O Sacrum Convivium, *163*

Prayer Index

Padre Pio's Prayer to His Guardian Angel, *49*

Prayer of Adoration, *117*

Prayer of Consecration, *132*

Prayer of Daniel, *57*

Prayer of St. Anselm, *18*

Prayer of St. John Paul II to Mary, *108*

Prayer of Thanksgiving, *118*

Prayer of Thomas à Kempis, *2*

Propagation of the Faith, *135*

Regina Coeli, *16*

Sacred Heart of Jesus, *171*

Seven Gifts of the Holy Spirit, *133*

Stay With Me, *141*

Students, *6*

St. Michael Prayer, *50*

Sub Tuum Praesidium, *102*

Surrender to God, *5*

Sweet Jesus, *154*

Thanks Be to Thee, *122*

That All May Know God in Truth, *26*

The Angelus, *94*

The Glory Be, *xiv*

The Jesus Prayer, *71*

The Sign of the Cross, *xi*

The *Trisagion*, *29*

To Be Conformed to the Holy Spirit, *27*

To Do God's Will, *12*

To Know and Love God, *4*

To Love Someone, *85*

To Mary, Undoer of Knots, *99*

To St. Joseph, *185*

To the Holy Spirit, *40*

Traditional Prayer Before a Crucifix, *127*

Traditional Prayer to Angels and Saints Before Mass, *165*

Trinitarian Selection from the Nicene Creed, *32*

Unity, *176*

Upon the Time of Death, *194*

Veneration of Mary, *104*